RACE

TO THE BOTTOM OF THE

EARTH

SURVIVING
ANTARCTICA

RACE
TO THE BOTTOM OF THE
EARTH

SURVIVING ANTARCTICA

REBECCA E. F. BARONE

SQUARE
FISH

HENRY HOLT AND COMPANY

New York

ANTARCTICA

INTERNATIONAL BOUNDARY

0   500   1000 Miles
0   500   1000 Kilometers

SQUARE
FISH

An imprint of Macmillan Publishing Group, LLC
120 Broadway, New York, NY 10271 • mackids.com

Our books may be purchased in bulk for promotional,
educational, or business use. Please contact your local
bookseller or the Macmillan Corporate and Premium
Sales Department at (800) 221-7945 ext. 5442 or by email at
MacmillanSpecialMarkets@macmillan.com.

Library of Congress Control Number: 2020021758

Originally published in the United States by Henry Holt
and Company
First Square Fish edition, 2023
Book designed by Kay Petronio
Square Fish logo designed by Filomena Tuosto
Printed in the United States of America by Lakeside Book
Company, Harrisonburg, Virginia

ISBN 978-1-250-86607-3 (paperback)
10 9 8 7 6 5 4 3 2 1

LEXILE: 940L

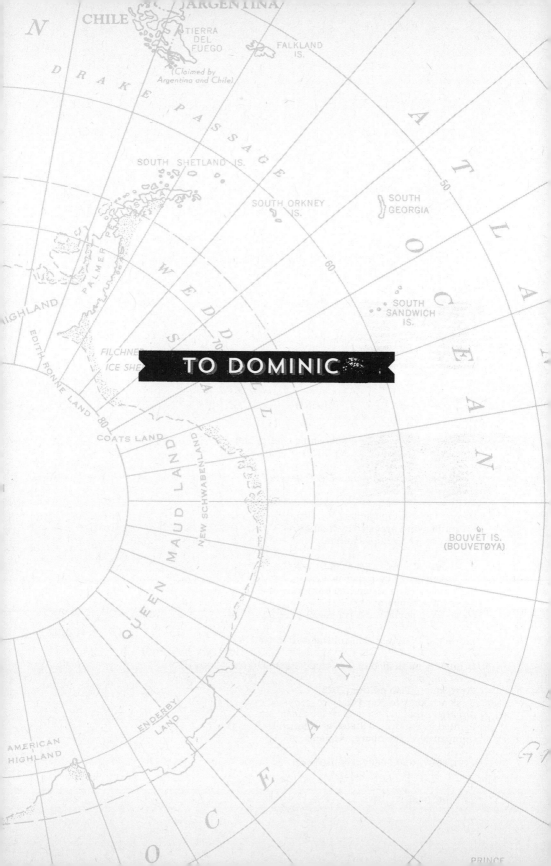

TO DOMINIC

CONTENTS

Amundsen/Scott
Antarctica routes
1911–1912

Scott's
Route

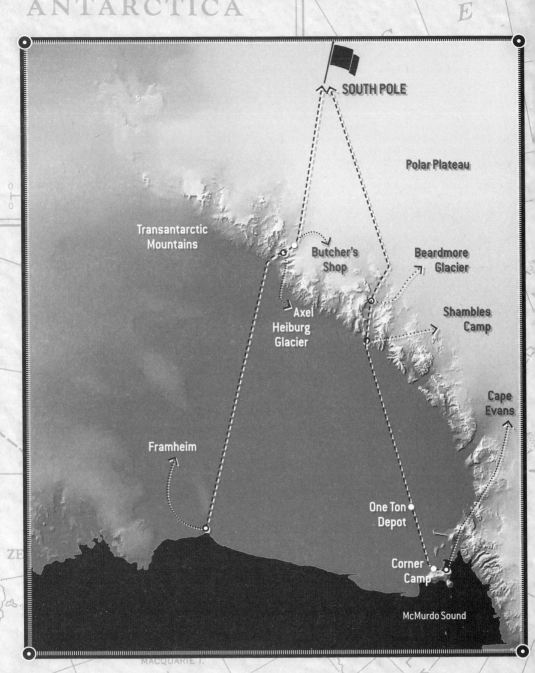

ANTARCTICA

SOUTH POLE

Polar Plateau

Transantarctic
Mountains

Butcher's
Shop

Beardmore
Glacier

Axel
Heiburg
Glacier

Shambles
Camp

Cape
Evans

Framheim

One Ton
Depot

Corner
Camp

McMurdo Sound

Amundsen/Scott Antarctica routes 1903–1910

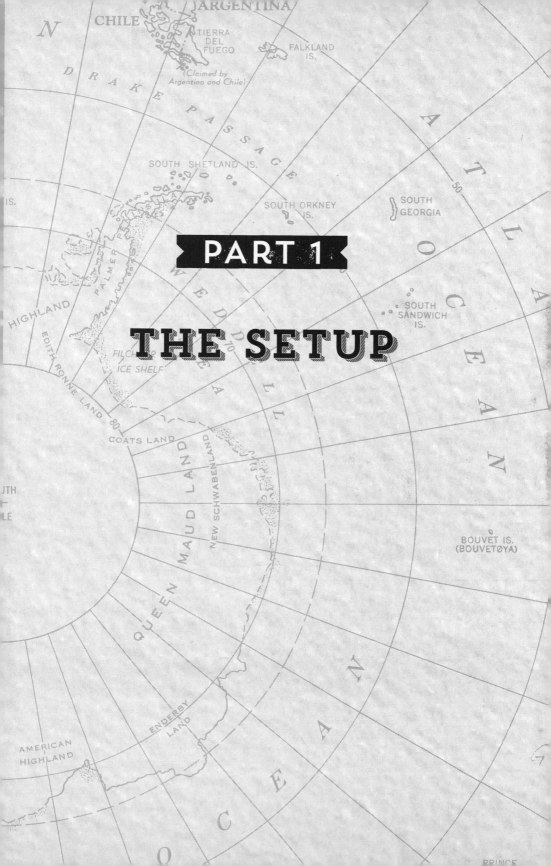

PART 1

THE SETUP

"I write the history of the South Pole! If anyone had hinted a word of anything of the sort four or five years ago, I should have looked upon him as incurably mad. And yet the madman would have been right. One circumstance has followed on the heels of another, and everything has turned out so entirely different from what I had imagined."[1]

—Roald Amundsen, April 13, 1912

"So here we are practically on the summit and up to date in the provision line. We ought to get through."[2]

—Captain Scott, December 21, 1911

CHAPTER 1

THE RACE,

AMUNDSEN/SCOTT: 1903-1910

London, England—1906

Captain Robert Falcon Scott couldn't shake the darkness. There had been celebrations and honors, parades and royal invitations, but joy was beyond his reach. His gloom was inescapable. Bare, stark, and numb. So much like the Antarctic desert that he had abandoned, summoned home before he could reach his target.

Scott had turned back before reaching the South Pole.

In 1903, he had journeyed farther south than anyone had ever before. He had gone to Antarctica and traveled 960 miles across the ice, trying to reach the South Pole. Because of him, England's flag was closer to the pole than any other in the world.

But he had missed his mark. To the nation he might be a hero, but in his own eyes he had failed. He hadn't gone far enough.

It had been the dogs. He had taken dogs, had intended for them to pull sleds across the ice and up glaciers. Dogs were supposed to be hearty. They were supposed to eat half of what a man did but pull almost as much. They were supposed to respond to orders and mind their human masters. They were *supposed* to. But it hadn't worked out that way. "It is odds that the dog rather than the man directs the walk," Scott had lamented.[3] The dogs had turned on him and turned on one another. In the end, the men had ended up hauling the dogs.

It had been the men, too. They all went snow-blind. Bright sunlight reflected off the ice and snow and burned the men's eyes. At one point, there was only one working eye among the three people who made the push to the pole. They recovered, somewhat, but then scurvy made them weak and confused. The men could have been better prepared. If only Scott had known then what he knew now.

He had been so close, only 8° away. He had almost made it. *Almost.*

He had to go back.

It began in whispers. He wrote to a friend, tossed out the idea as if it was just a casual, passing thought: maybe he would try again. Just a hint, a suggestion, a quick note in a letter once or twice that laced possibility to the edge of his sadness.

Robert Falcon Scott (1905).
[Henry Maull and John Fox/Wikimedia Commons]

Then it began to build. What if, Scott mused, he took motorized vehicles to Antarctica? He had been a torpedo officer in the Royal Navy; machines made more sense to him than animals. He began to ask a few trusted officers from his last expedition—did they think polar cars could help a team reach the South Pole? Could this be his vindication? Their emphatic yes was all Scott needed. Hope had taken hold and given direction to his darkness.

Quickly then, it grew. Friends, former expedition members, and explorers of all kinds offered help. In 1906, not even two years after his return, Scott decided to embark on a second trip to Antarctica. This was his opportunity, his chance to triumph, where before he had failed.

Work started at once on the polar motorcars. In Paris, France; Birmingham, England; and Fefor, Norway, great polar explorers and engineers began designing machines. But, in the middle of his planning, Scott was called back to his ship in the Royal Navy, "forced to reinstate myself and get some experience before I again ask for leave."[4] Though he had sailed on great royal yachts from the time he was thirteen years old, he suddenly felt trapped and claustrophobic. "I am dreadfully sick of this [naval] routine," Scott wrote to his sister.[5] He wanted news, and he raced into every port, eagerly searching for updates from his team.

It took years of designing and redesigning, testing and retesting. In the end, an entirely new vehicle emerged: the motor sledge. Wolseley Motors from Birmingham, England, created a gas-powered crawler with an innovative concept of looped treads in place of wheels. Scott and his wife went to see the final tests in person, ardently hoping that these could be "the key to everything," he wrote.[6] On the long, snowy slopes of Fefor, the motor sledges easily pulled heavy loads up the mountains.

Sure, they had a way of breaking down unpredictably. Sure, they were heavy. But they weren't dogs.

Still, he would take dogs, and ponies, too, just in case. Perhaps this new group, he thought, perhaps these dogs would be equal to the task. If the motor sledges broke, then the ponies could haul. If the ponies grew sickly, then the dogs could work. And, there could be no greater prize than reaching the pole through the purest form of all: man-hauling as they had before.

Scott wrote that "no journey ever made with dogs can approach the height of that fine conception . . . when a party of men go forth to face hardships, dangers, and difficulties with their own unaided efforts . . . Surely in this case the conquest is more nobly and splendidly won."[7] Dogs and ponies could be useful, but man-hauling was the ultimate in honor. This time—this time!—the men would be better prepared.

Scott's two expeditions were less than a decade apart, yet knowledge of how to live and work in polar conditions had changed dramatically. Now, they knew to eat seal meat—fresh and plentiful in

Man-hauling in Antarctica. Sledges were pulled by teams of two to five men.
[Wikimedia Commons]

the Antarctic waters—to ward off scurvy. No one knew exactly why or how it worked, but eating fresh meat seemed to ensure that people stayed healthy.

Traveling would be different, too, even beyond the motor sledges. In Norway, Scott had ordered fifty pairs of custom-made skis. The best skis, with the most advanced bindings in the world, would help them over the ice. Their eyes would be better protected this time as well. With dark goggles, they wouldn't have to fear the sunlight on the snow. Scott put every bit of polar knowledge to work.

In 1909, Scott made his official announcement. His goal was clear: "The main object of the expedition is to reach the South Pole and secure for the British Empire the honour of that achievement."[8]

Scott had no problem finding volunteers for his crew. On his first return from Antarctica, the nation had cheered. For his second venture, it seemed like all of Britain wanted to be part of his glory. When he announced the Antarctic expedition, more than eight thousand people applied to join his crew on the three-year journey. He chose sixty-five.

Many were seamen and officers, on loan from the Merchant Marines or the Royal Navy like Scott. They had all volunteered to go. Scott needed men who would watch with constant attention while sailing a ship around ice floes. He needed people with strength to build shelters, perseverance to maintain the base camp, and dedication to simply survive the long, dark polar winters. The expedition demanded courage, but almost more so, it demanded passion. Once they left civilization, there was no escaping the dark and cold. Not a man among them could have second thoughts; there was no turning back.

Twelve of the crew were scientists: physicists, geologists, biologists, and zoologists. Antarctica, especially the interior where the South Pole lay, was entirely unknown. Scott was excited about a research program that aimed to collect meteorology data, study penguin mating habits, and collect fossils of ancient plants that may have once grown where ice now reigned.

A few other members of the crew were neither sailors nor scientists. Bernard Day, an engineer who helped design and test the motor sledges, was aboard for vehicle maintenance and to make improvements along the way. Two eighteen-year-old Russians were hired to drive the dogs, a groom was brought on to tend to the ponies, and a champion Norwegian skier was hired to teach the men how to ski in Antarctica.

Then there was Apsley Cherry-Garrard. He didn't apply for a defined role. He simply was so excited about the expedition that he had paid Captain Scott £1,000 to buy his way aboard. At first, Scott had refused. But, when Cherry-Garrard told Scott to keep the money anyway, the goodwill won him a spot on the voyage.

It was a big expedition, hardly a nimble strike force that could move quickly. But Scott had prepared for a long-term expedition rather than a quick dash to the pole.

In June 1910, they boarded the *Terra Nova* in Cardiff, Wales. She was a three-masted whaler already tested in the icy Antarctic waters and a steal at only £12,500 (less than half the cost of the *Discovery* from Scott's first polar expedition). In the docks, alongside great cargo ships and liners, she looked small and uninspiring. But in the Antarctic waters, she was a powerful fighter. Seven feet of wood reinforced her hull. Scott had already seen her grinding and crushing her way through ice and knew she was equal to the task. She would get them to Antarctica.

With the crew, basic supplies, and motor sledges aboard, they settled in for the journey. From Cardiff they would sail to Cape Town, South Africa, then on to Melbourne, Australia, and Lyttelton, New Zealand, for additional supplies.

All sixty-five men knew the risks they were taking. Perhaps Scott had been to Antarctica and back safely, but plenty of others had paid the ultimate price along the way, never to be seen again. As the *Terra Nova* prepared to depart Cardiff, Scott ordered the entire crew to write their wills.

They left, each man knowing his duty yet blind to whether he would ever return home.

They were off. Headed south.

S

Christiania (Oslo), Norway—1907

Roald Amundsen had always loved the ice. He wanted, craved, the prizes of sacrifice. Suffering, endurance, hunger. The greater these hardships, the greater the resulting victory.

He was a tall, muscularly framed man with a long, stern face that hid any secrets. It was a face that could take rain as easily as sunshine and wither a lesser man with a single glance. Roald Amundsen was destined to explore the frozen, dark desert. Roald Amundsen dreamed of the North Pole.

Growing up in Norway at the end of the nineteenth century,

Roald Amundsen (1908).
[Ludwik Szaciński/Wikimedia Commons]

Roald had always looked north. Young Amundsen was transfixed by the stories of daring explorers who sacrificed everything for adventures in the frozen ice worlds of the very northern seas. Even as a child, he exercised and worked his muscles, developing them to endure what the ice would demand. The Arctic was waiting, and Roald couldn't grow up fast enough.

"Whatever I have accomplished in exploration," Amundsen later recalled, "has been the result of lifelong planning, painstaking preparation, and the hardest of conscientious work."[9]

By the time he was thirty-five years old, in 1907, he was an expert skier, a certified ship's captain, a natural leader, and already an Arctic explorer with experience skiing across one of Norway's mountain plateaus in the dead of winter. Roald had no trouble convincing anyone that he could be the first person to the North Pole. Raising the necessary funds, however, was a different story.

Money slowly trickled in. Bit by bit, though, with donors often contributing out of a sense of patriotism, Amundsen began to scrape enough together to put a down payment on a ship and hire a crew.

The ship, the *Fram*, was built specifically for polar exploration. She had been designed by a team of three renowned polar explorers. The sheathing over her hull was built so that it would be torn off rather than fractured in the ice; this way, the *Fram* stayed watertight, allowing it to avoid cracks and gashes that would slowly sink her. As another safety feature, the hull itself was curved so that ice would lift the ship, rather than crush it. (However, she was nausea-inducing on the open water. She rolled wildly over the easiest swells, a side effect of all these efforts to prepare her for the ice. Her critics snidely remarked that "she is not adapted for very heavy seas, and may turn turtle [roll over]."[10]) For Amundsen's expedition, her steam power was

The Fram in dry dock. Her curved hull, the structure built to contact the water, is shown held by white braces. The bow, or front, of the ship is pointing out of the page.
[National Library of Norway]

replaced with an internal combustion engine, making her the first polar ship to have diesel power.

The crew, too, was chosen with one goal in mind: to reach the North Pole before anyone else. With only nineteen men aboard, every one of them needed to know how to handle the ship, handle the ice, and handle the fatigue of darkness during the six-month winter. Next to knowledge and fortitude, Amundsen chose his crew based on their ability to keep a positive attitude. Amundsen knew within minutes of talking to a man if he would succeed as part of his expedition or not.

But then, in 1909, with Amundsen just months away from setting sail, newspapers around the world began screaming the names of Frederick Cook and Robert Peary.

One of them, or both of them—it wasn't entirely clear—had reached the North Pole. Amundsen could not be first.

"This was a blow indeed!" Amundsen later said.[11] But he wasted no time grieving for the record that would never be his. Almost as soon as he heard the news, he began to think of a new plan. "If the expedition was to be saved," Amundsen later wrote, "it was necessary to act quickly and without hesitation."[12]

The North Pole had been claimed, but the other side of the world was uncharted. If the North Pole couldn't be his, then the South Pole would be. Secretly, Amundsen decided to challenge Captain Scott—who had already announced his expedition—to the South Pole.

No one else knew it yet, but Scott's expedition would not be alone in Antarctica.

Plans would have to be made fast, and they would have to be made in the utmost privacy. "Everything had to be got ready quietly and calmly," he wrote.[13] Amundsen had barely raised enough money to try for the North Pole; if investors heard he had changed plans, they would certainly withdraw their support.

Amundsen didn't even tell his own crew that their destination had changed.

The first thing he did after deciding on his new goal was to order one hundred Greenland dogs. Dogs, he was convinced, "were the only practicable draught animals for use in snow and ice. They are quick, strong, sure-footed, intelligent, and able to negotiate any terrain that man himself can traverse."[14] They weathered the blinding sun and the cold well. And, if they had to, they would eat other dogs as food.

There was a certain magic about them, a personality and dynamic that made handling the dogs as much of an art as leading people. "The dog must understand that he has to obey in everything," Amundsen later wrote, "and the master must know how to make himself respected."[15] He didn't understand Captain Scott and the reluctant English attitude toward dogs. It was their loss.

But other than putting in an order for the dogs, nothing else in public view seemed to change. Arctic provisions were still bought. Arctic—not Antarctic—maps were still laid out. The crew still held for their original launch date. Outwardly, Amundsen kept to his stated goal of going north and publicly refocused the expedition on completing scientific research rather than exploration at the North Pole.

He told only one person of the change in plans: his brother Leon, "upon whose absolute silence I could blindly rely."[16] As the expedition's manager, Leon could be counted on to make the last-minute changes and alert the right people at the right time and not a moment before. Roald Amundsen trusted no one else.

The *Fram*, with Amundsen and his crew, set sail on August 9, 1910.

They followed their original plan to resupply and do final outfitting of the boat in Madeira, Portugal, before heading north to the Arctic.

It wasn't until three hours before their departure from Madeira—their last port of call before heading into the unknown—that Amundsen called his crew together. Though they grumbled at being disturbed from writing their last letters home and making their own final preparations, they gathered to hear what their leader had to say.

With his men all assembled in front of him, Amundsen spoke. They were headed south, he said, aiming for the grand prize of first to the South Pole—not the silver prize of second place to the north.

The men were stunned. It took them several moments to understand what he had said. Then, they began to cheer.

Amundsen didn't trust it. Celebration and excitement were good, but shallow emotion could fizzle as quickly as it arose. It was easy to be caught in a moment's anticipation; it would be much more difficult to weather the hard years ahead.

One by one, Amundsen pulled each man aside. He asked them, individually, if they would like to leave. They were each given an opportunity to resign without any repercussions.

"As the names were called, every single man had his 'Yes' ready," Amundsen remembered.[17] Not a single man quit.

The *Fram* set sail for Antarctica on September 9, 1910.

Leon saw them off from the docks in Madeira, and then he got to work. The brother that Roald had trusted to keep silent was now about to send three of the most important messages of his life. One went to Amundsen's mentor, apologizing for keeping his true goal a secret. One went to the press, announcing the challenge for the South Pole. And one message, a telegram, headed farther south.

S

Melbourne, Australia—1910

The *Terra Nova* sailed into Melbourne, Australia, on October 12, 1910. The crew was light and joking after the easy passage from South Africa. After this, all that was left was a quick trip to New Zealand to pick up the ponies and then on to the ice. Scott's crew was a team, happy to be working together and looking forward to the years they would spend on the frozen desert. They were in it for the long haul.

Letters and mail waited for Scott that followed any leader of an expedition. Bills to be paid, sponsors and fans asking for updates and advice, and orders for supplies to be sorted through. It was routine, expected, and familiar.

Until he opened a single telegram.

"BEG LEAVE TO INFORM YOU FRAM PROCEEDING ANTARCTIC—AMUNDSEN"[18]

Scott had settled in for a siege.

Now, it was a race.

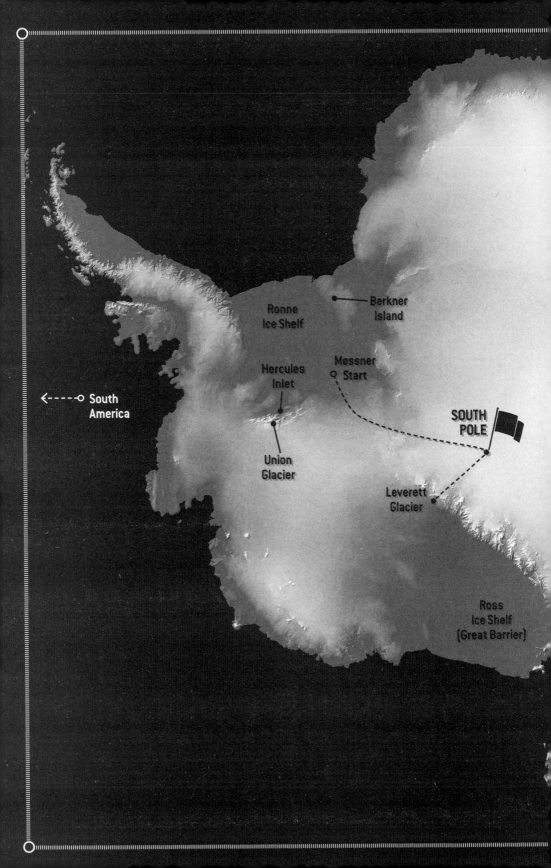

Berkner
Island

Ronne
Ice Shelf

Messner
Start

Hercules
Inlet

←----○ South
America

SOUTH
POLE

Union
Glacier

Leverett
Glacier

Ross
Ice Shelf
(Great Barrier)

Lou/Colin
Antarctica route
2018

"I know the journey ahead will be more challenging than anything I've ever experienced but that struggle is what will make the joy of the finish line even sweeter."

~Colin O'Brady, October 16, 2018 [19]

"I am under no illusions as to the enormity of the task."

~Lou Rudd, April 1, 2018 [20]

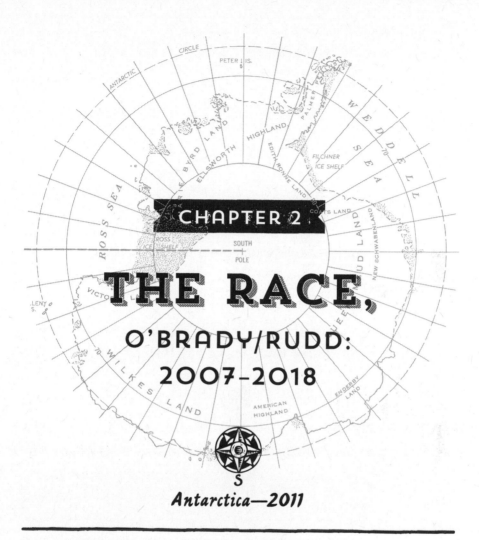

CHAPTER 2

THE RACE,

O'BRADY/RUDD:
2007-2018

Antarctica—2011

In the space of a heartbeat, everything can change. Hundreds of miles from the nearest person, on the driest, windiest, highest continent on Earth, Englishmen Henry Worsley and Lou Rudd had no one but themselves to depend on for survival. Every move and every decision had consequences.

It was the summer of 2011 in Antarctica. They had stopped for a break from their work hauling polar sleds called pulks across the ice. Lou had gotten out the canteen and a cup, just as he had done during their journey so many times before.

He had forgotten about the wind. The wind could kill.

A gust rose up, and, in the flash of a moment, the wind caught the stream of water as Lou poured from the canteen. The water spilled, soaking his glove and drenching his hand underneath.

Henry rushed to his side. They had to get Lou dry. His skin had already frozen, and seconds mattered in saving his hand. Quickly, they wiped away every drop of water with whatever cloth was nearest.

"Get wet, you die." Henry had said it before, and he said it again now.[21] It wasn't the last time that he would teach Lou how to survive at the very bottom of the earth.

Lou was in great shape; they both were. He had excelled at all the cold-weather training, and, at home in England, he had read all of the books and training manuals and instructions about venturing into the Antarctic. But the thin line between life and death rested on experience more than book learning; nothing could take the place of practice.

Henry was the seasoned expert, and Lou was the novice. For weeks they skied, climbed glaciers, crossed mountains, and skirted crevasses. Lou soaked it all in, falling in love with "the sheer vastness of Antarctica," he said, and learning everything he could from the best leader.[22] "I knew absolutely nothing about polar travel; the dark arts, the routines, the kit," Lou recalled. "He [Henry] taught me everything."[23]

But just five years later, Henry Worsley was dead.

In 2016, Henry had tried to traverse Antarctica—crossing from one end to the other—alone, unsupported, and unassisted. Only 110 miles from the finish, he collapsed, in too much pain to go farther. For two days he lay in his tent, too weak to even boil water, hoping against hope that he could continue on. But his strength never returned, and his mind started to follow his body's unraveling. Finally, in a moment of lucidity, he called for rescue. He was flown to Chile for emergency surgery, but it was too late. He died in the operating room.

Henry had tried to do the impossible, people said. Only six people had managed to traverse the continent on foot. "More people have walked on the moon (twelve) than have traversed Antarctica," Lou wrote.[24] And none had ever crossed alone, unaided, and unsupported. Perhaps it just couldn't be done.

Henry Worsley, a mentor and friend to Lou. His death from an attempted solo, unsupported, unaided traverse of Antarctica spurred Lou to take on the 2018 solo, unassisted, unsupported crossing.
[National Museums Liverpool/Wikimedia Commons]

"Unsupported" meant Henry had carried everything he needed with him on the pulk. Every bit of food, every liter of fuel, every piece of clothing, backup gear, emergency equipment, and any little item of comfort. When he passed the research base full of scientists at the South Pole, he couldn't even accept a tissue or a cup of tea.

"Unaided" meant he traveled under his own power. Mile after mile, through violent headwinds and up 10,000 feet of elevation, he alone, without any help, had pulled his pulk. No sails, no kites, and certainly no powered vehicles. The only way forward was with his own feet.

For men like Lou, Henry was a mentor, a friend, an inspiration. It was his enthusiasm that shaped their expeditions, and it was his

Captain Lou Rudd (2018). [René Koster Photography]

knowledge they relied on to conquer each obstacle. His death stunned them all.

Through his grief at his friend's death, Lou planned another trip of his own. Like him, the whole team would be composed of soldiers from the British military. Lou would lead the team of six men to finish the journey that Henry had started, a traverse of Antarctica. They would mostly follow Henry's route, but, unlike Henry, Lou's team would travel together and resupply at the South Pole. It wouldn't be the solo, unsupported, unaided expedition that Henry had undertaken, but it would be a memorial to a hero.

Lou's five companions were eager and athletic, but "they were polar novices, some had never been on skis," Lou said.[25] They trained and studied, just as Lou had. And Lou taught them, just as Henry had taught him.

When they reached the Transantarctic Mountains where Henry had spent his last days, Lou and his teammates climbed to a peak with a brilliant view. Here, in a place that Henry had loved, they held a memorial service for Lou's dear friend. As they came down the mountain, Lou watched his compass, the very same one that Henry had used, letting his friend guide him once more. They reached the far side of the continent twelve days later. They had finished, for Henry.

Lou understood why Henry had come back, again and again, even in the face of great danger. Antarctica was unlike anywhere else in the world. There was loneliness in its vast, empty wasteland of ice and wind. But there was loneliness in leaving it, too.

"Like a siren song," Lou explained, "she draws you back."[26]

One year after Lou's return, Ben Saunders, an accomplished British polar explorer, set out to make his own attempt at the solo, unaided, unsupported crossing. He had also known Henry and dedicated the journey to his memory. But Ben never finished, either. At the South Pole, he realized the remaining thirteen days of food left in his pulk weren't enough—the finish was at least seventeen days away. The best way to honor Henry, he decided, was to come home alive.

"Impossible," people kept saying, kept labeling the lonely crossing. It wasn't called that out of respect for those who had failed. It wasn't labeled that as a taunt for those that might attempt it, either. A solo, unaided, unsupported crossing of Antarctica seemed impossible, because no one knew if the equation between the weight of the pulk and the food needed for survival could ever be solved.

Food is heavy. The more weight you carry, the more energy you burn. The more energy you burn, the more food you need and the more fuel you need to prepare that food. Which means more weight to carry. And on and on and on. No one knew if it was humanly possible to survive for long enough on the food and fuel that one man could pull behind him. "It's right at the limits," Lou said.[27]

Yet Lou couldn't stop thinking about Antarctica. There was opportunity in the challenge; he saw it just as Henry had. In leading his last expedition, Lou had traversed Antarctica, something Henry had never done before attempting the record. Lou knew the terrain. He knew the environment. The more he thought about it, the more he realized that he was set up for success. His experience, the invaluable knowledge that could only come from living and doing, was unlike anyone else's.

Henry had died, leaving a record unset; Lou would see it finished. Lou was going back to Antarctica. He would see his treasured land of ice and wind, and he would raise money for The Soldiers' Charity, honoring veterans and their families. Each step he took would help others. He would do some good while doing the impossible.

Lou threw himself into training. He was on active duty in the British Army, and he prepared in the early hours before work and in the late nights after he came home. Along the banks of the River Wye, he pulled giant Land Rover tires behind him, harnessed to his body just like the pulk would be. For hours at a time, with his dog scampering alongside, he pulled the tires over dirt and gravel and bumpy hills. The more difficult the terrain, the better, as he towed a "20 kg tire through quite long grass."[28] He switched it up every few days, going to the gym to train lower body strength with dead lifts and squats and off-road racing on his bike for cardiac endurance.

In the spring, he headed to Greenland, pulling a pulk on skis and honing his reflexes on the ice sheet. Greenland was the next best thing to actually being in Antarctica, and there was always more to learn.

As a tribute and a blessing, Henry's widow gave Lou the Worsley family crest. He would carry it for courage and fly it at the finish in triumph.

As the UK summer cooled into fall and the winter darkness began to lighten in Antarctica, Lou made final checks to his pulk and ate his last meals at home. Then, as much as he had been counting down the days, it seemed to suddenly appear: October 2018. It was almost time to leave.

He was ready to do the impossible.

Washington, United States—2018

For Colin O'Brady, there was a Before, and there was an After.

Before, he had taken life for granted. Before, his mom had nicknamed him "Mr. A-minus."[29] Before, he had never done more than the bare minimum needed to win.

He won a lot. He was a high-performer, so naturally smart that he skipped third grade. He started swimming competitively at five years old, and by the time he was a teenager, he was nationally ranked in two sports: swimming and soccer.

He was talented—really talented!—so, what was the point of doing more than necessary? If he could do minimal work and receive an A-, he reasoned, then why bother doing extra work just to score a little higher and get an A? It drove his coaches and teachers crazy. Over and over he heard, "Don't you know how good you could be, if you only tried your hardest?"[30] He just couldn't quite see why he should bother.

He looked at life differently, After.

After meant challenging himself every day. After meant inspiring others, not just winning for himself alone. After meant never taking health—life—for granted, ever.

In 2006, Colin took all the money he had made from painting houses for the past six summers and set out to travel around the world. He took his surfboard and a backpack, looking for adventure and fun, determined to say yes to everything.

On the remote island of Koh Tao in Thailand, he said yes to fire jumping, a dazzling celebration of light and fun in the dark of night. Up and down the beach, tourists and locals took turns skipping rope. Except this rope had been soaked in kerosene and lit on fire.

Colin only took a few jumps before it went "terribly wrong," he later remembered.[31]

Usually, if someone tripped, the rope would simply bounce off their body. But when Colin stumbled, the rope didn't peel away. The flaming cord twisted around his legs, trapping him and wrapping him in fire.

Fire jumping on a beach in Thailand. [Nika Vee/Flickr]

Kerosene washed over him, soaking his clothes and drenching his skin, as flames laced over his body from his feet to his neck.

"Instinct takes over," he later said.[32] Somehow, he remembered the ocean.

He ran 10 feet to the waves, extinguishing the flames in salt water that ate into his raw flesh. The last thing he did before shock racked his body was to look at his friend and plead, "Help."

The fire was out, but the damage was done.

He had eight surgeries in eight days. Second- and third-degree burns covered 25 percent of his body, stripping his legs of skin and severely damaging the tendons of his knees and ankles. Even if he made it through without life-threatening infection, the doctors told him he would never walk, much less run or swim, the same way again.

It was "the darkest time of my life," he said.[33] "It was like so much of my identity had been taken away from me."[34]

They moved him to world-class facilities in Bangkok, and the surgeons were stellar. The risk of infection went down with each day. He would live.

But, if it hadn't been for his mom, he might never have recovered.

She flew to Thailand five days after the accident. Though she was terrified and grieving for her son's loss, she never let him see her cry. The minute she opened his hospital door, all Colin saw was optimism. "Let's stay positive," she kept insisting, always upbeat and maddeningly cheerful.[35] She was convinced he could heal, that his body would do what his mind instructed.

The key was to visualize who he wanted to be. Every day, she asked him about his future: "Let's set a goal together," she said.[36] What did he want to do with the rest of his life? Who did he want to be after he got home? What was his goal, his dream? Legs aside—she didn't let him think of them—what did he want to do?

Finally, mostly to get her off his back, he tossed out an idea: a triathlon. When he imagined himself healthy with fully-functioning legs—as impossible a dream as that might be—he saw himself "crossing the finish line of a triathlon, which is not something I'd ever done before," he later said.[37]

It was just what his mom wanted to hear. Now, he had a goal. Now, she wouldn't let him off the hook.

They threw themselves into research, spending hours scouring the internet for information on distances, gear, races, and training plans. Colin's mom never let it feel like a wild dream. To her, they were working toward a reasonable, achievable ambition.

Even before his legs could handle any weight, Colin began training his arms in his hospital room. Later, he laughed to himself as he remembered, "I literally have this photo of me with the Thai doctor. I'm, you know, my legs are bandaged to my waist and the Thai doctor is like looking at me like I'm crazy but I'm lifting these like ten-pound barbells. In my head going, 'I'm training for a triathlon now!'"[38]

His mom already had his mind focused on what would come next. Colin's motivation for rehab, for taking his first step, for taking that first slow, agonizing walk outside, was always to get ready for a triathlon. Painful step by painful step, he had her voice in his mind.

Keep going. Keep at it. You can do it.

He repeated her words so often they became his own.

Until one day, he could not only walk but run. Then, one day, he started to train. He got stronger, faster, more agile. Before long, he was ready to compete.

Eighteen months after his accident, eighteen months after learning that he might never walk again like he had before the accident, Colin entered the Chicago triathlon, amid a field of four thousand competitors. Half a world and a seeming-lifetime away from the Thai beach where he very nearly died, Colin plunged into open water once more.

To his "complete and utter surprise," he didn't just compete—he won.[39]

After meant no more Mr. A-minus. After meant giving it his all, all the time.

Colin quit his job in finance the day after the race, and for six years he competed as a professional triathlete, traveling around the world for the US National team. Then, when he decided he needed a new challenge, he turned to breaking adventure records. In 2016, he summited the highest peak on each continent and skied the final degree to both the North and South Poles—the Explorers Grand Slam—in only 139 days, smashing the previous record by 53 days.

His mother had been right. The burns had not been hopeless, and he had recovered. It had been hard work, at times seemingly impossible, but he overcame. Colin had found the key to success: what counts is the voice you choose to listen to, which mantras you take as your own.

It was staggering what mental strength could do. When Colin found himself climbing Denali, the highest peak in North America, only a hundred hours after summiting Everest, every ounce of his energy went to convincing himself he could make it. If his brain was convinced, his body would follow. Over and over, he repeated: "You're strong. You're capable." And when the pain threatened to overwhelm him: "This too shall pass."[40] His body would always do what his mind instructed.

Around the world, people lined up to hear about his adventures. With every story he told and jaw-dropping picture he showed, he demonstrated the power of mental strength. He told them that they, too, had the strength within them to overcome whatever challenges they faced. That consciously telling your brain messages of resiliency and courage would help make resiliency and courage a reality. He challenged his audience—in every auditorium and every classroom: What impossible goal do you want to achieve?

It was a question he returned to again and again. What was his body, his *mind*, capable of?

Henry Worsley had passed through the South Pole only days before Colin arrived there during the Explorers Grand Slam in 2016. Colin knew Henry's journey was unfinished. He knew, too, of Ben Saunders. He knew their goal had been left unaccomplished.

It was one thing to set world records, but it was another thing entirely to do what had never been done. Alone. Unaided. Unsupported. An impossible challenge.

Colin O'Brady (2016). [Colin O'Brady/Wikimedia Commons]

Colin refused to believe it.

The crossing of Antarctica would test every fiber of his strength, both mental and physical. There was the very real possibility of failure, and in Antarctica, failure could be the last thing he ever did. Despite the risks, it was the perfect challenge for him, and it would be the perfect way to inspire others to take up their own challenges, too. He just couldn't pass it up.

Quietly, without attracting attention or notice, he began to make plans.

Climbing mountains and hiking kept him in peak shape. To hone his body, to adapt it and perfect it to the unique rigors of Antarctica, Colin added weight training to his regimen. All of his exercises were designed to add muscle mass. In any long expedition in Antarctica, weight loss would be inevitable. He gained weight, adding pound after pound, saying that "you have to put on weight knowing you're going to lose weight."[41] The more he added now, the more he could stand to lose.

Even during the physical training, he worked to build and keep his mental edge. Colin and his trainers "would do cardio until my heart rate was at a peak state," Colin explained, and then "have me wall sit with 45 lbs. of weight on my knees and my feet in ice buckets."[42] As fatigue made his body shake and his brain fuzzy, Colin fought to assemble Legos, struggling to manipulate the tiny pieces with trembling fingers and to follow instructions with his tired mind. Mental strength would always have to be more powerful than physical strength. He made a habit of using his mind to overcome situational discomfort.

By the end of the summer, Colin knew he had the necessary power. But, there was no substitute for rehearsing with his gear and pulk on the ice. So he added a trip to Greenland to his already packed schedule. Throughout the trip, Colin kept a live journal for his 65,000+ followers on Instagram, posting beautiful pictures, and writing about overcoming obstacles and keeping his mind calm when faced with the unexpected.

Still, no one knew that this trip was anything but another adventure for the sake of adventure. Colin didn't give any clues that skiing across Greenland was part of something much bigger.

Then, on September 14, 2018, as his Greenland expedition came to an end, Colin broke his silence. "I came here to train for the most ambitious and difficult project of my life," he wrote. "I'M READY! Announcement coming soon on the new project."[43]

But just what this new project would be, Colin didn't say.

London, England—October 17, 2018

October 17, 2018, was a big day for Lou Rudd. In full military dress at Buckingham Palace, he accepted a medal and honor from the queen for his success with the army team in Antarctica.

As if the award wasn't enough, that night he launched his new expedition with a party in London. He had raised more than $200,000 to fund the trip, in addition to the money he had raised for charity. Sponsors, friends, relatives, and coworkers came to celebrate the start of an adventure. Everyone listened as he stood on a stage under a bright spotlight and described the journey one last time before setting off to attempt a historic first.

It had been a big day, and it had been a big night.

It wasn't over yet.

Thousands of miles away, another adventurer was set to have a big night of his own. On Instagram, Colin O'Brady posted his most extraordinary update ever:

"ANNOUNCING THE BIGGEST PROJECT OF MY LIFE: 'THE IMPOSSIBLE FIRST' . . . On November 1st, I depart for the ice."[44]

Within minutes, it was favorited thousands of times. The world knew.

Captain Rudd wasn't the only one aiming to make the first solo, unaided, unsupported crossing of Antarctica.

Now, it was a race.

"Strangely enough the thing . . . that appealed to me most strongly was the sufferings [Arctic explorers] endured. A strange ambition burned within me to endure those same sufferings. . . . Secretly—because I would never have dared to mention the idea to my mother, who I knew would be unsympathetic—I irretrievably decided to be an Arctic explorer."

~Roald Amundsen, 1927[45]

"My story . . . shows how curiously the course of one's life can be turned."

~Captain Scott, 1905[46]

CHAPTER 3

THE BEGINNING,

AMUNDSEN/SCOTT:
1890–1909

London, England—June 1899

Captain Robert Falcon Scott had never planned to go to Antarctica.

By his own account, Scott wrote, "I may as well confess at once that I have no predilection for Polar exploration."[47] He had never loved the ice or the cold, and later he would fill journals with descriptions of the "awful" land at the end of the earth.[48] But in 1899, just one day after his thirty-first birthday, and only two days after hearing about the position, Scott applied to lead the first British expedition to Antarctica.

He never explained why. But whatever pushed him to take the job, to go so far away, must have been powerful.

Perhaps he wanted fame. In the early twentieth century, polar exploration led headlines. Returning captains were lauded as brave, daring men and given awards and adulation on speaking tours that made them rich. Money could have been very attractive.

Or, maybe the reason was more personal.

Perhaps he needed to get away, far away, to move past tragedy. His father and brother had died fourteen months apart, both unexpectedly. Now he alone was financially responsible for his mother and unmarried sisters. The paycheck from the expedition to Antarctica would help support them, and no one could blame him for wanting to leave the hard year far behind.

And yet, it could have been that he wasn't trying to escape ghosts as much as he was trying to run from himself. Scott had fought depression, dark, black days when he could barely get out of bed, all his life. Antarctica could be a change, a new start, a chance to be someone different in a far different place. Perhaps darkness would be different at the bottom of the earth.

Whatever the reason why he volunteered, Scott was chosen to lead the British voyage of 1901 to Antarctica on the ship *Discovery*.

Never, not once, was reaching the South Pole written as a goal. The closest was an instruction that "geographical exploration should be directed to . . . an advance to the south."[49] Yet an electric current ran through every conversation Scott had with his sponsors; they all wanted to claim the last reaches of the earth for Britain. The expedition's purpose was for science, not record-breaking. Yet Commander Scott knew, without being told, that he would make a run for it.

The expedition left London on July 31, 1901. Crowds lined the banks and cheered as the *Discovery* sailed down the Thames. Twenty-three weeks later, the crew reached Antarctica.

For hundreds of miles, Scott sailed along the Great Barrier (renamed Ross Ice Shelf in 1953). Rising sometimes 200 or 300 feet in the air, the Barrier was a vertical wall of ice that separated the ocean from the unknown. "The very vastness of what lay at our feet seemed to add to our sense of mystery," wrote Scott when he first saw it.[50]

For nearly a month, Scott sailed in search of solid ground. In Antarctica, the sun disappeared behind the horizon at the start of winter in April and did not return until the spring, in August. No one could venture away from camp in the deep cold that followed the onset of night and winter. All exploration stopped until the spring, and Scott needed safe, calm ground on which to build a shelter.

On a rocky shore near the calm bay of McMurdo Sound, Scott finally found a stretch of open ground. The crew built a hut for the men

The Great Barrier/Ross Ice Shelf on the right at the Bay of Whales. The dark spots in the lower left-hand side are people, and the modern-day icebreaking ship Nathaniel B. Palmer *is in the center. [Michael Van Woert/Wikimedia Commons]*

and shelter for the animals. Through the long polar darkness, they waited for the sun to reappear.

When spring returned, the push to the pole was the disaster of dogs and snow blindness and scurvy (discussed in Chapter 1) that haunted Scott. But, while their journey failed to reach the pole, teamwork and comradery were a resounding success. Scott took two other men with him—Dr. Edward Wilson and Ernest Shackleton—in his pursuit of the pole, and soon both men would be famous: one for living and one for dying.

They journeyed south until scant food and fuel forced them to turn back. They could see mountains ahead, but they were unable to find a way past deep gashes in the ice called crevasses that fenced them in. Then, when Shackleton began to show signs of scurvy, he stumbled on for as long as he could.

The hut at Hut Point, Scott's base during the Discovery *expedition, as it stood in 2012.*
[Sergey Tarasenko/Wikimedia Commons]

Shackleton, Scott, and Dr. Wilson before starting south on the Discovery *expedition (Nov. 2, 1902).*
[Wikimedia Commons]

"We determined," Scott wrote, ". . . to push on to our utmost limit."[51] Neither Scott nor Wilson ever complained about carrying Shackleton when he eventually collapsed.

When they returned to base camp, their relief ship, carrying food and supplies, was anchored at the edge of the harbor. Yet no matter how much fresh food and rest Shackleton enjoyed, his health just would not improve. Against Shackleton's protests, Scott made the hard decision, "to the regret of all of us," he wrote, to send his friend home with the relief ship's departure.[52] It was just too hard to recuperate in Antarctica.

For another year, Scott and his men went out on other journeys across the ice. But their goal was never again the pole. They had tried and failed; there was too much else to explore, too much else to do, to attempt it again.

At the end of that third year, Scott was summoned home, and he announced the end of the expedition to the rest of his men with tears in his eyes. Whatever his initial motivation to lead the expedition, Scott left Antarctica with sadness.

But as Scott was just beginning his return, Shackleton had already arrived back in London. He was the first to come home, and he was the first to leave again in search of the South Pole.

In 1908, Shackleton returned to Antarctica and headed to the pole once more. This time, using ponies instead of dogs, he and his team raced over the wide expanse of the icy Great Barrier and managed to find a path through crevasses and jagged fences of ice called pressure ridges that separated them from the mountains.

They followed a long, wide glacier for more than 120 miles, up more than 8,000 feet through the Transantarctic Mountains to the high polar plateau, naming the pass Beardmore Glacier. The sledge runners flew over the slick blue ice as if this route had been created for their one purpose.

However, at the top of the glacier, the polar plateau was a different story. With the team winded in the thin air and suffering from altitude sickness, dwindling rations forced Shackleton to turn back only 112 miles from his goal. He had been so close, but because of his brave decision to retreat, every one of his men made it back safely.

Shackleton hadn't reached the pole, but he had found a way there. Back in London after his return, he wrote and spoke freely about all he had found, publishing his discoveries in the expedition's report and passing on his maps so that others could follow. The whole world now knew how to get to the very bottom of the earth, and Scott was determined to go back.

Example of a crevasse—a deep, wide crack in the snow or ice. [mountainstroh/Flickr]

Scott added Shackleton's knowledge to his own experience, and made plans for the motor sledges. Everything seemed different for his second expedition. This time, he knew what he was facing. This time, he was prepared.

Christiania, Norway—1890

Roald Engelbregt Gravning Amundsen's mother wanted him to stay home. She wasn't subtle: go to school, get a job on land, and stay close. Roald's father and three older brothers had all gone to sea as merchants; she wanted something different for her youngest son.

He couldn't disappoint her, not as the youngest of the family, not when she asked so plainly and openly. As much as he desperately wanted to explore, at eighteen years old, he agreed to stay in Christiania and study medicine.

Yet even as he went through the motions, he was always looking for ways to train and prepare for adventure at the North Pole. While he (barely) passed his exams, he "insisted on sleeping with my bedroom windows wide open, even in the bitterest weather."[53] While he (half-heartedly) applied to medical school, he spent evenings and weekends skiing in the mountains, "increasing my skill in traversing ice and snow and hardening my muscles for the coming great adventure."[54] While he (mostly) went to lectures, he "read all the books on the subject [of Arctic exploration] that I could lay my hands on."[55]

He was a dutiful son, and he genuinely mourned his mother when she passed away during his second year at college. But he quit school the next semester.

Even with Roald's newfound freedom, the life of an Arctic explorer still almost escaped him. For years, he wrote letters introducing himself to leaders of different expeditions. Letter after letter after letter was rejected. No one wanted a man without experience, and he couldn't get experience without someone hiring him.

Anyone else might have given up. Roald refused. It took three years, but he finally was accepted, without pay, on a Belgian expedition heading to Antarctica. It was as far from the North Pole as he could get, but Roald leaped at the chance to serve on a real expedition.

The journey was a disaster. The captain and first mate, through ineptitude or ignorance, locked their ship into polar ice so that they had no choice but to weather the Antarctic winter. The men did not have proper clothing or food, and the entire crew nearly starved. The isolation and terror of constant darkness amid dangerous icebergs combined with the devastating effects of scurvy led two men to go insane.

Disgusted with the incompetent leadership, Roald left at the first port they came to. From then on, he decided, he would lead, not follow. His years of letter-writing and begging were over. Inadequate preparation, authoritative command, crew disunity—they had nearly doomed that first voyage. Amundsen swore his expeditions would never fail because of these.

With only a few more quick trips in the waters around Norway, he accumulated enough hours to qualify for a sailing master's certificate. He didn't waste any time. In his newly minted title of "captain," Roald announced plans to navigate the Northwest Passage.

For more than five hundred years, people had tried and failed to find a sea route from the Atlantic to the Pacific using the Arctic Ocean, north of the North American continent. The maze of inlets and archipelagos were unmapped, and towering icebergs and shallow channels with sharp rocks threatened any ship that might try to slip through. The Northwest Passage, Amundsen wrote, was a "baffling mystery to all the navigators of the past."[56] The Arctic waters were famous for their wrecks, with crews resorting to mutiny and cannibalism in attempts to survive.

The first explorer to find the elusive path would have his name etched in history books. It was exactly the adventure—the challenge, the uncertainty, the promise of hardship and suffering for the chance at a momentous reward—that Roald longed for.

Starting what would be a trend for the rest of his life, Roald was heavily in debt by the time he was ready to cast off. He had managed to raise some money, but it seemed like there was never quite enough to go around. Creditors were prowling the very docks where his ship, the *Gjøa*, was moored when he raced off at midnight under the cover of a furious storm.

In spite of the dramatic launch, the rest of the transit to Canada was peaceful. Though Roald's goal was the Northwest Passage, the meager funds he had been able to raise were dedicated to Arctic research. Before he could pilot a course through unmapped waters, he would be forced to spend two years taking magnetic and meteorological readings while anchored in northern Canada, in a small bay they christened "Gjøa Haven."

Yet Roald was stubborn enough to force even this delay to work to his advantage. He intended to learn all he could about living in polar environments from the people who knew best: the land's native population.

Only two weeks after the *Gjøa*'s arrival, five men slowly appeared over the horizon. Amundsen and his men rushed out to meet them.

The two groups stopped, separated by a small field, each eyeing the strangers.

Amundsen gathered his courage and shouted: "TEIMA!"

He had read from the memoirs of other explorers that "teima" meant hello in the local language, and he had carefully coached his crew on what to say. Soon, his men followed suit, and yells of "teima!" "teima!" "teima!" were loud in the air.

Men on the deck of Gjøa.
[Library of Congress]

The native men were utterly bewildered, and they stood still, staring at the strange men. Then, after a moment, they continued forward, all of them in turn shouting "manik-ut-mi!"[57]

For all of his effort, Amundsen had taught his men the wrong language.

Thankfully, both sets of men understood the other's welcoming intent, if not the actual words. The two groups became and remained friends for the whole of Amundsen's stay. These five native men passed along the word, and other tribes came and made camp at Gjøa Haven as well.

It seemed like each meeting brought new knowledge to the Europeans, and Amundsen desperately wanted the skills for thriving in the cold that the natives took for granted. The Netsilik taught them how to make the sledge slide easily over the snow by coating the bottom-most part, called the runners, with ice. Often, the crew of the *Gjøa* traded for the natives' reindeer-skin clothing, which was warmer and more comfortable than the clothing they had brought with them. Amundsen later wrote that the Netsilik "fur garments were the most suitable for this climate."[58]

The Netsilik snow houses, too, beat European tents when the weather fell to its coldest. Amundsen managed to convince his friend Teraiu to teach him how to build. Every afternoon, Amundsen and his men practiced as "Old Teraiu . . . shook his head pensively, evidently in the conviction that we had taken leave of our senses. Sometimes he would throw out his arms to indicate the overwhelming number of houses, and exclaim, 'Iglu amichjui-amichjui-amichjui!' Which means, 'This is a dreadful lot of houses.'" To Amundsen, it wasn't waste; it was survival training for the future.

The Netsilik taught Amundsen and his men valuable polar survival skills.
[National Library of Norway]

Amundsen and his crew spent two years anchored in the little harbor. Far from wasting this time, he had set himself up with some of the best tools imaginable to aid his survival in polar climates.

Back on the water, in August 1905, Amundsen and his crew inched the *Gjøa* along the dangerous Arctic Archipelago through the elusive Northwest Passage. Jagged rocks just centimeters below her hull threatened to rip gashes into the wood, and fog blinded them in water that had never before been charted—or seen—by Europeans.

For the last three weeks of the journey, when the water was at its shallowest and the danger at the greatest, Amundsen recalled, "I could not eat or sleep. Food stuck in my throat when I tried to swallow. Every nerve was strained to the limit in the resolve to foresee every danger and to avoid every pitfall."[59]

Finally, after three weeks of trudging along, they saw another ship, one coming at their bow, not their stern. "What a glorious sight that was—the distant outlines of a whaling vessel in the west!"[60] Amundsen wrote. The ship had come from the Pacific, and the rest of their way was clear. Amundsen's planning—using a small crew on a small boat that was maneuverable—and his leadership had succeeded where everyone else had failed. They had made it, had become the first westerners to sail from the Atlantic to the Pacific in the Arctic. Amundsen was a hero.

Slowly, Amundsen made his way back to Norway, making long stops in the US and England for speaking tours and interviews. He had conquered what had been left undone for centuries, and he received a celebrity's welcome at every stop. But the lessons of the Netsilik were never far from his mind. The Northwest Passage had been the dream of a child, and he had realized his boyhood hope.

It was time for bigger dreams.

"When it's blue sky and you're on the polar plateau, you can feel so small. It's just endless, and you're like this tiny little speck. You can look 360 degrees, there's nothing. There's no tree, no building. You are the only tiny little thing out there in this endless sea of light."

~Colin O'Brady, January 2019 [61]

"It's a place that can kill you in minutes if you get things wrong. It could be as simple as pitching your tent, if the wind catches it . . . it's gone, it floats like a parachute and blows away. Potentially life-threatening situations can develop in seconds, especially when solo. . . . You've got to be either daft or courageous, or probably a bit of both!"

~Lou Rudd, October 2018 [62]

CHAPTER 4

THE BEGINNING,

O'BRADY/RUDD: SPRING–FALL 2018

Hereford, England—Spring 2018

Lou had been dreaming of Antarctica since he was twelve years old.

One day, while sitting in the principal's office, waiting to be punished for causing trouble in math class, he picked up a thin, pale-blue book with five men on the cover planting a brilliant Union Jack—the British flag—on top of a snow-covered hill. The book was *Captain Scott: An Adventure from History*. The world disappeared around him as Lou was caught up in the race to the South Pole half a century earlier. "I was blown away," he said, "absolutely gobsmacked by this epic journey." He finished it and knew: one day, he promised himself, he would see Antarctica, too.[63]

But he wasn't about to wait around for adventure to come to him—he sought it out. At fourteen years old, Lou rode his bike, alone, from his mom's house in England to his dad's house in Scotland—a journey of more than five hundred miles, just to prove that he could. Then, when he was sixteen, he joined the military and spent almost thirty years serving tours of duty in Kosovo, Afghanistan, Iraq, and Norway, becoming an expert in security and Arctic warfare. He married and had three children. There was excitement and challenge at every turn.

Yet, for all of this, he never stopped thinking about Antarctica. He was always looking, always searching, for an opportunity that might take him there.

Finally, one day in 2007, he saw a magazine ad from fellow soldier Henry Worsley seeking teammates for an Antarctic expedition. Without ever having seen the ice or set foot there before, Lou was so convinced that he was going to love Antarctica that he replied to Henry's application to man-haul for hundreds of miles. "That was the first opportunity I had," Lou remembered, "and it was really straight into the deep end with quite an extreme trip."[64]

Lou was the novice, and Henry was the expert (as recounted in Chapter 2). Lou trained and read and prepared at home as much as he could, anxiously waiting for the departure date. Then, just months before the start, Lou was called up for deployment to Afghanistan.

So, Lou went to the hot, scorching desert, determined to keep training for the freezing, windy desert. He took his pulk harness and found big off-road tires just like the ones he used to practice hauling while back home in England. For six months, whenever he could eke out a bit of time from his regular duties, he wound his way around the perimeter of Kandahar Airfield over and over and over, pulling his tires in the dust. "We're sharing a base with a lot of other nationalities, Americans and Canadians, and they'd all be heading out in their vehicles on patrol and coming past me and they'd all be comments like, 'Hey, that looks like a bit of a drag, mate,'" Lou joked about his strange exercise.[65] But no amount of teasing could make him give it up. Antarctica was his dream.

His deployment ended only one week before the expedition began. From Kandahar to Antarctica, he traded one desert for another—with a change in temperature of almost 180°F!

Antarctica was stunning, raw and untouched. "It's so vast and desolate," Lou said, "you really feel like you are out there alone pitching yourself against the challenging conditions. There's nowhere else like it on the planet."[66] It was a place for reckoning and finding out what was truly at your core. The dream he had kept alive for so long was even better in reality than in his imagination.

Of course he would be going back after that first expedition. It was hardly a question in his mind. Once the lure of the ice caught hold, it didn't let go.

He had returned a second time with teammates to memorialize Henry, but now Lou's third trip would be different—solo, a record-breaking first that no one had ever managed to complete. Success was anything but certain. Henry Worsley had died. Ben Saunders had admitted defeat. They had been experts, hardly amateurs or un-tested gym athletes. But at the bottom of the world, death comes more naturally than life. How could Lou succeed where the others had failed?

Lou couldn't hope to improve on Henry or Ben with conditioning or strength. Besides, he had man-hauled his pulk on both of his previous

Antarctic mountain range. [Christopher Michel/ALƐ]

expeditions; he knew how to get in shape. It didn't seem like success or failure would ride on a change in his training program.

His food regimen, too, he thought he had perfected. At best, he could only hope to haul the weight of 6,000 calories per day, even as he anticipated burning 10,000 calories per day or more. Every single day, he would consume only two thirds of the energy he would expend. On his last expedition, six-foot-tall Lou had lost thirty-six pounds.

For the 6,000 calories, Lou knew what worked for him: 1,000 calories of creamy porridge in the morning. Then at night, he would eat a freeze-dried meal, a heavy dessert, and an energy shake. All day long while hauling, Lou would also eat his way through a grazing bag full of broken bits of macadamia nuts, energy bars, cheese, and salami.

"Every hour," Lou explained, "you'd just grab a handful of it and just pop it in your mouth and just keep your calories constantly coming in."[67] In the beginning, before the exhaustion really set in, he wouldn't be able to eat everything. By the end, he would eat it all and still go to bed hungry.

Lou knew what it felt like to slowly starve in Antarctica. He was prepared to feel that pain. Yet, to be successful, something had to change. He couldn't repeat what Henry and Ben had done and still hope to realize a first. Lou's training, experience, and nutrition were locked in. The only major factor left was the route.

Route-planning an Antarctica expedition was complex. First, large sections of the continent were filled with deep, wide rends in the ice called crevasses, with sheer sides and black voids that seemed to stretch into nothingness, littering the ground for hundreds of miles. In Antarctica, the ice was always moving as old crevasses closed and new ones ripped open throughout the year. Routes had to be chosen to minimize the danger of encountering a crevasse.

Then, starting and ending points had to be accessible to planes as well as pulks. Lou would be flown from the Antarctic base camp to his start point and then from his finish back to the base camp; the plane had to be able to land.

Finally, for a traverse of the continent, there was the very definition of Antarctica itself to contend with.

Antarctica was covered in ice. In some places, the ice, which formed as glaciers over land, pushed out for hundreds of miles over water in sections called ice shelves. These ice shelves were massive. To the west of the Antarctic Peninsula, the Ross Ice Shelf (called the Great Barrier until 1953) was nearly the size of France. On the opposite side of the continent, the Ronne Ice Shelf was almost as big and nearly 500 feet thick. Even sitting above water, this ice still felt as solid as dry ground.

Tents for a camp between Hercules Inlet and the South Pole, the route that Lou Rudd and his team took to memorialize Henry Worsley. [Carl Alvey/ALE]

Was Antarctica defined by the edge of the ice shelves or the edge of rocky ground (called a landmass)? It was a big question: What defined a crossing of Antarctica?

In the end, Lou decided that a traverse of Antarctica meant crossing over the ground, not over the entire expanse of the ice sheet. He had started at the edge of the landmass in 2016, and he would start in the same place once more: Hercules Inlet. It was easy to reach by plane, and he was already familiar with the terrain.

As for the finish, Lou knew exactly what he was *not* going to do. In 2016, Lou finished his journey at the bottom of Shackleton Glacier, and he vowed never to do it again.

Shackleton Glacier was riddled with crevasses. Again and again, several times a day, the ground disappeared from under him as he fell through the ice. Each time, he was saved by the rope connecting him to the anchor of his pulk and the quick work of his teammates. It was a scary situation in a group. It was downright dangerous for anyone traveling alone.

The Leverett Glacier, on the other hand, was a far safer option. Along the length of the glacier—from the South Pole and out past Lou's finish line to the edge of the Ross Ice Shelf—the US National Science Foundation maintained the South Pole Overland Traverse (SPOT) path. It was hardly more than a well-traveled section of ice, but it meant that all the crevasses along the glacier had been filled in and the ice was being watched carefully as more developed.

"As a husband and father of three," Lou explained, "safety was always my utmost priority with this trip."[68]

He decided: Hercules Inlet to the base of the Leverett Glacier via the South Pole. It was a hybrid of places he knew and the safest routes to take, with all the hallmarks of a successful first.

As a last piece of strategy, Lou decided to announce his attempt early. His polar experience and planning might scare off any would-be competitors ready to challenge him for the record-breaking "first." It was time for Lou to stake his claim.

On April 1, 2018, he posted to his website: "As a fitting tribute to the legacy of Henry I am hoping to go to Antarctica to complete his journey."[69] Now the world knew.

For months, no one seemed to be ready to challenge him. But almost halfway around the world, Colin O'Brady was making his own plans in secret.

Portland, Oregon—Summer 2018

Colin was almost as different from Lou as could be imagined. In the summer of 2018, Lou was forty-nine; Colin was just thirty-three. Lou had made a career out of service in the military; Colin was a professional athlete and adventurer. Lou had already made two successful, long-distance expeditions to the South Pole. Colin had been to Antarctica only once, and he had skied only the last degree, sixty-nine miles, to the pole. They saw the same challenges and opportunities, but they looked at the world from completely different views.

Their strategy and preparation were as different as their backgrounds.

Colin, too, realized the advantage of defining Antarctica by its landmass. But, he reasoned, wouldn't it make more sense to put the glacier and its dramatic elevation change at the beginning, rather than at the end? When he was fresh and still strong, he could go up through the mountains, quickly gaining almost 10,000 feet to the polar plateau in just a few days. If he were to tackle the glacier at the end, this opposite direction would mean spreading out the climb over more than an agonizing month.

In fact, the first woman to traverse Antarctica, Felicity Aston, had traveled in this direction as well. She had scaled the difficult altitude early on, and with two resupply drops to help her, she had set the record.

The big difference, though, was that Felicity wasn't racing anyone.

At the base of the Leverett Glacier, blizzards, high winds, and dangerous drops in temperature were wildly unpredictable until early December. Any of those conditions could keep the plane from being able to fly him to the start. And while Colin waited, Lou would already have begun in the opposite direction. (The weather was more certain at Hercules Inlet.) It was a big bet, guessing that the strategic elevation advantages would outweigh a long-delayed start.

Colin's finish, on the other hand, was an easy decision: the landmark Messner Start was one of the most-used points for expeditions heading to and from the South Pole. It was also the closest edge of the landmass to the South Pole. Colin knew he would be racing Lou; he would use all the advantage he could get.

Colin's route was set: base of Leverett Glacier to the Messner Start via the South Pole. He was just going to have to gamble on good weather.

Food, on the other hand, was something that Colin never left to chance. Good, organic food would absolutely fuel his journey. But asking his body to haul hundreds of pounds for months on end in an inhumane environment meant that every calorie had to count. He turned to science for help.

For years, Colin had used the nutritional supplements and food produced by a company called Standard Process to fuel his competitions. Now, he asked them to develop something entirely new: the perfect food, tailored exactly to the specific characteristics that his body, and no one else's, needed.

Over the course of almost a year, Colin underwent a full battery of aerobic and anaerobic testing. In the Human Performance Lab at Appalachian State University, scientists measured his peak power and capacity on a bike and a treadmill, his grip strength, his pull strength, and his standing jump height. Colin sat in his swimsuit and

Colin O'Brady with his pulk and gear. [TAMARA MERINO/New York Times/Redux]

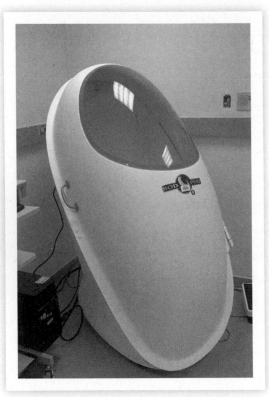

The Bod Pod, which measures body composition. Colin used scientific equipment to optimize his nutrition plan for the coming race.
[National Institutes of Health/Wikimedia Commons]

swim cap inside a Bod Pod, an egg-shaped capsule that looked like a miniature rocket ship, to very precisely measure the composition of muscle and fat on his body. All these data provided baseline measurements to determine how Colin's training, and the food he ate during that training, affected his fitness.

Henry Worsley had died from an infection in his intestines, and the scientists at Standard Process guessed that his immune system had suffered from extreme stress and attacked his gut by mistake. In an attempt to avoid the same fate, Colin underwent more than two hundred blood tests to provide scientists with information as to which foods showed even the slightest hint of an inflammatory or allergic response in his body. "Because your body's under so much stress out there," Colin later explained, "we're trying to find out what would burn the absolute cleanest."[70]

In the end, Standard Process developed an entirely new energy bar: the Colin Bar. It was plant-based, full of cranberries, dates, chia seeds, pumpkin seeds, pea protein powder, nuts, and held together with coconut oil and all subtly flavored with cocoa powder. "They're quite good," Colin later declared of the bars.[71]

It was the first of its kind: custom-made food to fuel a journey that would be the first of its kind as well. At 1,250 calories each, four a day plus oatmeal for breakfast, ramen for lunch, and a freeze-dried meal at night with protein powder and chicken soup would provide all of his planned 7,000 calories.

Colin's training was as unique as his choice of route and his food. In addition to working physically and mentally in the gym, he continued breaking records outdoors. In June and July of 2018, he set the record for the 50 Peaks Challenge by summiting the highest point in every US state in only twenty-one days.

Through it all, he posted updates and took his Instagram followers along with him. His mission, even during training, was to inspire others to overcome challenges and to move their own bodies more.

"This journey isn't just about me," Colin posted on Instagram, "but more importantly about unlocking the untapped potential that lives inside all of us."[72]

As he traveled from state to state to climb the highest points of each, he invited locals to come out and hike with him, be it for a mile, a day, or an entire climb. Colin never kept his desire to inspire a secret. The only thing he kept under wraps was his next big project.

With route, food, and training settled, there was just one more component to Colin's strategy: the element of surprise. If no one knew what he was planning, no one could second-guess him or try to imitate his tactics. Only at the last minute, right before he left for Chile, would he announce the Impossible First project, his biggest attempt at record-breaking yet.

Colin was ready. All that remained was Antarctica.

"Every day we had occasion to bless our ski. We often used to ask each other where we should now have been without these excellent appliances. The usual answer was: Most probably at the bottom of some crevasse."

~Roald Amundsen, November 29, 1911[73]

"There is rather an increased condition of false crust—that is, a crust which appears firm till the whole weight of the animal [pony] is put upon it, when it suddenly gives some three or four inches. This is very trying for the poor beasts. There are also more patches in which the men sink, so that walking is getting more troublesome . . ."

~Captain Scott, November 22, 1911[74]

CHAPTER 5

THE SETUP,

AMUNDSEN/SCOTT: DECEMBER 1, 1910–APRIL 1911

Off the coast of Antarctica—December 1910

Captain Scott insisted that his strategy had not changed: he had always been determined to be the first to reach the South Pole. A race was aggravating but immaterial. He was an impatient man; he was already going as fast as he could.

It was a cruel joke, then, when the slushy ocean of small ice and water turned to hard, fast pack ice. "We are captured," Scott wrote in his diary, as the *Terra Nova* was trapped in a standstill.[75] Sailing was useless, and even pushing on with their steam-powered engines would be a "sheer waste of coal," Scott wrote.[76]

For three long, agonizing weeks, they simply sat. "I can imagine

Early 1900s ship trapped in Antarctic pack ice. [Frank Hurley/Wikimedia Commons]

few things more trying to the patience than the long wasted days of waiting," Scott wrote. "To wait idly is the worst of conditions."[77] The men went out onto the ice floes and practiced skiing. They watched penguins playing and sliding on icebergs. But none of it brought them any closer to the South Pole.

Finally, on December 30, they fought through the maze of sun-warmed paths of open water between ice floes and were free. The *Terra Nova* "behaved splendidly—no other ship . . . would have come through so well," Scott wrote as he set a course for McMurdo Sound, just as he had with the *Discovery* expedition.[78] On January 4, 1911, he found the perfect spot for a base camp thirteen miles north of the *Discovery*'s old home and christened it Cape Evans, in honor of his second-in-command, Teddy Evans.

Men and animals, grateful to be released after the cramped sea voyage, raced to set up camp. Ponies and two teams of dogs made a continuous circuit from the ship to the building site and back again, off-loading supplies. Two of the three motor sledges were up and running, too. (The third unfortunately sank while being brought off the ship. No one was hurt.) Each motor sledge required an engineer to mind the continuous series of breakdowns, but Scott was pleased with the good loads they hauled.

Henry Bowers, a skilled lieutenant, kept an almost encyclopedic knowledge of the content and location of each box in his head. Only eight days after landing, the entire ship had been unloaded, and, five days after that, the crew had moved inside the hut, now standing fifty feet long, twenty-five feet wide, and nine feet tall. "The hut is becoming the most comfortable dwelling-place imaginable," wrote Scott.[79]

It was a beautiful, inspiring time. The promise of adventure and the hope of victory next summer at the pole spurred them on. Dr. Wilson, who had again come with Scott to Antarctica, wrote in his journals, "The peace of God which passes all understanding reigns here in these days."[80] He spent hours with his watercolors, and the men often begged him to draw a scene that had brought them to stillness with its beauty.

While the supplies were still being organized and the finishing

One of Scott's new motor sledges, showing the crawler treads designed for use on the snow.
[Herbert Ponting/Wikimedia Commons]

touches put on the hut, Scott directed the men to begin preparing for the depot-laying trip. By stocking food and fuel at strategic points along the way this season, the teams could carry less next summer during the race. Their goal that summer was a major supply base at 80° south—690 miles from the pole—with smaller stores leading to that point.

It was up to Bowers to organize it all, and he took it in stride with energy that was becoming legend. Never missing a beat, he unloaded the *Terra Nova* with one list and packed for the coming trip with another. Added to these regular duties, he also volunteered to lead a pony on the depot-laying trip. By the time the team left, he hadn't slept in seventy-two hours.

In itself, the depot-laying trip was a small thing. They wouldn't be going far, and it was hardly risking life or limb. But everyone knew the journey was a dry run for the race next summer. Anyone who hoped to go to the pole needed to make the first cut: the depot team.

Scott alone had made the decision of who would come. Some of his choices were obvious. Cecil Meares, the chief dog handler, was clearly going to lead one of the dog teams. Titus Oates, the groom, who "was

Dr. Wilson, Bowers, and Cherry-Garrard recuperating from a perilous midwinter journey.
[Wikimedia Commons]

perfectly excellent and untiring in his devotion to the animals," Scott wrote, was going to lead one of the ponies.[81]

A few of the crew were repeat volunteers from the *Discovery* expedition. Dr. Wilson and Teddy Evans were known, trusted, and valued by Scott. Thomas Crean's powerful build, too, would come in handy for man-hauling. All three men would certainly lead their own ponies.

Others, though, were a surprise when Scott announced his decision. Bowers had risen so high in Scott's esteem that he made the cut. Apsley Cherry-Garrard, too, was unexpected, but Scott had come to see strength in the man who had tried to buy his way onto the expedition. These were choices made from experience—Scott allowed individuals, both officers and sailors alike—to show their strengths and rise in his regard. He was undemocratic in his decision-making, but he never carried a grudge.

On January 26, 1911, Scott made a quick farewell speech to thank the entire expedition for their "splendid work. They have behaved like bricks and a finer lot of fellows never sailed a ship," he wrote.[82] Then he left with his team of twelve men, twenty-two dogs, and eight ponies.

The dogs were broken into two eleven-dog teams, each hauling sledges filled with 490 pounds of supplies, while each pony was given a 590-pound load. Of the entire 5,700-pound cargo, only 12 pounds per person were allotted for personal items, including clothing.

From the start, the ponies had a rough time. On the Barrier, the snow was deep and soft. The dogs raced ahead just fine, but the heavy ponies sank down over and over. As soon as they were safely away from the edge of the ice, Scott decided to stop and make the first drop, calling this Safety Camp.

They called the drops "depots," which was a fancy word for nothing more than "just a cairn of snow in which we buried food and oil,

A camp from Scott's expedition with dog teams and tent. The circle in front of the sledge on the left is a sledge-meter. Scott's and Amundsen's teams used the sledge-meter to measure their mileage. [Herbert Ponting/Wikimedia Commons]

over which a flag waved on a bamboo [stick]," noted Cherry-Garrard.[83] The depots were not elaborate, but in clear weather on the endless white horizon, they could easily be seen for miles.

Slowly urging the ponies on, they traveled east around fields of crevasses before heading due south. They made another drop at this turn, which they named Corner Camp.

The drop had come just in time, too, because no sooner had they set out their supplies than a blizzard began to rage. Inside their tents, the men were warm and comfortable; Cherry-Garrard even insisted that "sometimes a blizzard is a welcome rest."[84] But, outside, snow pelted in all directions, flying into a chaos of white driven by a frenzy of winds.

The ponies were nothing short of miserable. They had shed their winter coats when the *Terra Nova* had sailed through the tropics, and their thin, summer coats couldn't stand the cold. The blizzard lasted for four days and three of the ponies became so sick that they couldn't go on. As soon as the weather let up, Teddy Evans took the three animals and turned back toward Cape Evans. Every effort had to be made to save the ponies; they were too important for the journey to the pole next year.

Then, as if losing three of the ponies wasn't bad enough, through garbled instructions, the weakest of the remaining ponies was given the heaviest load. He fell farther and farther behind until he finally gave up and lay down in the snow. It was a vulnerable animal in a defenseless position, and the dogs attacked. Scott and the men beat them back with whips and sticks, but not before the dogs had torn the poor creature's flesh. The pony was so hurt that it couldn't haul. Four ponies, half the number that had started, were now out of commission.

The dogs—the vicious, feral dogs—were hungry and bored. The blank, white horizon was flat and changeless. Without anything to pull toward, they felt little reward for their days of hard work. They were being fed a lot, more than they would have been back at Cape Evans, but it was nothing compared to the debt made by pulling hundreds of pounds all day, every day. They did their work when blows and cursing made them, but it came at the price of savagery.

The ponies were failing, and the dogs were starving. It was obvious they wouldn't make it to 80°S without a drastic change.

Scott had to decide: Should he begin killing his ponies to use as meat, make it to his goal at 80°S, and place his hope entirely in dogs for next summer? Or should he retreat—make the final depot at a lower latitude and head back now, conserving the ponies for later?

In the end, Scott couldn't give up on his ponies. Ponies were what Shackleton had used, and that was reason enough for Scott to keep them alive. Next year, he argued, after they had time to grow thick

Scott had placed much of his hopes in these Siberian ponies. [Herbert Ponting/Wikimedia Commons]

winter coats, then they would be useful. He just couldn't bring himself to kill them.

The men laid One Ton Depot, the largest drop of all, thirty-six miles short of their goal. They set 2,181 pounds of food, fuel, and equipment inside a six-foot-high cairn, and started for home.

Raging winds and blizzards trapped them at Corner Camp, and the weak ponies now began dying. The journey out had made them feeble; the march back did them in. (The dogs, of course, were fine.) By the time the men trudged back into Cape Evans, only two ponies were alive of the eight that had started.

The trip had been a mess. They had laid supplies for next year, but they had fallen short of their intended site. The only positive side seemed to be that all the men had come back alive.

The blows didn't end there.

While Scott was gone, the *Terra Nova* went to explore the

little-known Bay of Whales at the eastern edge of the Great Barrier. He had no way of knowing it at the time, but as Scott was turning back from One Ton Depot, the *Terra Nova* was unexpectedly turning back as well. What they had found made Scott write in his journal that "every incident pales before" it.[85]

The sailors had reached the Bay of Whales, but they discovered another ship already anchored there.

They had found Amundsen.

The Norwegians were nearly finished off-loading supplies from the *Fram* when they saw the English *Terra Nova* cruise into the bay.

At the sight of Scott's ship, Amundsen and his men rushed their dogs down the ice at full speed, trying to impress the English crew. It worked. The sailors on the *Terra Nova* had never known that dogs could run as fast while pulling a sledge.

The two crews spent a few days together, eating meals on the *Terra Nova* and at the Norwegian base camp, Framheim. Aboard the *Terra Nova*, Amundsen and his men were horrified by the messy, dirty ship but were fascinated by the luxurious food and praised their hosts as "extremely kind."[86] For their part, the English crew was duly impressed with the dogs and skis of the Norwegians but took comfort that their motor sledges made Amundsen anxious. (They didn't let on that the motor sledges were often broken.)

Both crews learned, too, that neither carried any wireless technology. Not only would next year hold a race to the South Pole, but the first team to safely arrive back at the mainland would get to announce the winner to the world.

Soon, though, the *Terra Nova* moved on. They headed back to Cape Evans to relay Amundsen's location to Scott, leaving the Norwegians to prepare as best they could.

Bay of Whales, Antarctica—January 1911

Amundsen and the *Fram* had sailed into the Bay of Whales on January 14, 1911, after passing through the pack ice in only three days. They had started out later than Scott, and they had come through Antarctic seas after the pack had mostly broken up. No one knew the timing of ice formation and dispersion—it had been simple luck on Amundsen's part to find the ice that way—but he would take all the luck he could get.

In a lot of ways, like dog handling and his choice of clothing, Amundsen's experience in the Arctic helped him plan and prepare for the Antarctic journey. But, it wasn't everything. The area he'd explored in the north had nothing like the Great Barrier.

Amundsen had read every report and memoir about Antarctica that he could get his hands on. In all of Shackleton's writing, in all of Scott's reports, none had ever mentioned how men could scale a barrier of ice that rose 200 feet above sea level!

It was talked about in hushed tones that made it hard to separate legend from fact. "The mystic Barrier!" Amundsen recalled, "All accounts without exception . . . had spoken of this remarkable natural formation with apprehensive awe."[87]

The *GREAT BARRIER*: a vertical wall of ice, a discontinuity of water and solid surface. Clearly, Scott had managed to get to the top. Clearly, Shackleton had as well. But how?! With hope and maybe even a small prayer, Amundsen sailed to its base, trusting that he'd find a way.

When he got there, Amundsen and his men laughed. Their relief echoed around the bay as they came face-to-face with the Great Barrier. Yes, in some places the Barrier was 200 feet high, but in others it was a measly 15- or 20-foot little bump! And, right there in the Bay of Whales, right where Amundsen had planned to anchor, there was a ramp of packed snow "so that the ascent took the form of a little, gentle slope," Amundsen wrote.[88] The story of the Barrier had grown taller than the ice itself. Amundsen defeated a legend by simply walking a few steps up a ramp of good snow. They took it as an omen as good as any for their coming journeys.

Framheim (literally, "Home of the *Fram*") was a camp based on the Great Barrier. Where Captain Scott had decided to make his shelter on the firm, rocky ground of Cape Evans, Amundsen had chosen to risk making camp on the ice. Everyone on his crew agreed that rock would have made a better foundation, but there was no solid ground to be found around the bay. And Amundsen wanted the bay. It was as close to the pole, as far south, as a ship could sail, and it put them almost a full degree closer to the pole than Scott's team.

Amundsen did not dictate orders. A leader with absolute power had almost doomed his first voyage to Antarctica, and Amundsen knew better than to repeat those mistakes. As with every decision, he presented a plan, and then he talked it over with his crew. He laid out how the Bay of Whales would give them a significant head start, but he did not gloss over the risks. Each man had a vote when it came time to decide. In the end, they agreed that making camp two miles back from the edge of the ice would satisfy everyone.

With a campsite chosen and firm anchor set, it was the dogs' turn to work. Amundsen hitched eight dogs, some of his strongest and finest, to a sledge loaded with 600 pounds of equipment to take to

An artist's representation of men constructing Framheim. Pitched tents were used to shelter the dogs and for additional storage through the polar winter.
[National Library of Norway]

Framheim. He cracked his whip. He yelled. The sledge moved forward.

And then it stopped.

The dogs simply sat down and looked at one another in confusion. What could it mean, that they were expected to heave against this weight! "The dogs had spent half a year [on the *Fram*] in lying about and eating and drinking," Amundsen wrote, "and had got the impression that they would never have anything else to do."[89] The dogs had forgotten they were there for a reason.

By inches and yards, Amundsen and his men moved them forward, yelling, whipping, beating them as needed to make the dogs understand. It was harsh treatment and slow going, to say the least. In his head, Amundsen did a quick calculation and, at this pace, figured it would take his team almost a year to go from Framheim to the pole.

The dogs had to be made to go faster, to work harder. The whips came out over and over until the dogs were in shape once again. Amundsen and his men worked the dogs hard, pushing them to be the conquering force the men knew them to be.

Yet the men were anything but unfeeling. They knew each dog by its voice, and they knew just by listening if the dogs were hungry or love-struck or tired or playful. And when one dog was frostbitten after getting his leg wrapped in a harness, Amundsen himself spent thirty minutes soothing the paw, making sure he was all right. The dogs were as much a part of the team as any man.

As soon as the *Fram* was off-loaded and Framheim was reasonably settled, the depot journeys began. Just like Scott, Amundsen had decided to lay depots as far south as possible. However, rather than laying all the supplies in one trip, Amundsen planned a series of smaller journeys, switching out and refreshing dogs and men.

The first trip out was relaxed, with the dogs running well in the 12°F weather and enjoying the ice. Amundsen had left with three other men, three teams of dogs, and three sledges. The extra man who was not the master of a team skied in front of the dogs. This frontrunner broke the horizon, and, rather than pulling toward emptiness, the dogs chased the leader.

The next in line, the first sled, was the prime navigator, responsible for checking the lead man's course. Amundsen gave this job to Helmer Hanssen, his best dog driver. Hanssen had been with Amundsen on the *Gjøa*, and he had learned dog-driving from the best, the Netsilik. Every day, he broke the trail for the other dog teams and kept everyone on the right heading, never faltering even once.

They reached 80° south and laid down a stock of 1,650 pounds of pemmican (early energy bars made from dried meat or fish powder, animal fat, dried milk, vegetables, and oatmeal), seal meat, blubber, dried fish, margarine, and biscuits. The weather was excellent, the dogs pulled hard, and the men were filled with energy. Nevertheless, Amundsen kept looking for ways that things could go wrong.

Often on the journey out, a thick, gray muddling of the air—almost but not quite fog—had descended. The featureless horizon made the lone skier in front of the dogs constantly disoriented. "One can never be certain of one's surroundings," Amundsen wrote. "There are no shadows; everything looks the same."[90] It was only the quick course corrections by Hanssen that had kept them on track. They had found their way to the middle of nowhere, but finding it again would be far more difficult.

A single skier led the way, giving the dogs something to pull toward. The bindings around the skier's boots were advanced for the time. [National Library of Norway]

Route-finding was a problem Amundsen could solve, and he decided that they would mark their path on the way back. They started out using bamboo flags, and, when they ran out of flags, "our eyes fell upon a bundle of dried fish lying on one of the sledges, and our marking pegs were found," Amundsen wrote.[91] It was, he admitted to himself, probably the first road in the world marked using fish.

After racing back to Framheim, they quickly restocked and re-outfitted the sledges; time was never on an explorer's side in Antarctica. They left once again on February 22 with eight men, seven sledges, and forty-two dogs to lay a depot at 83° south, their longest trip of the season.

From the start, the second depot journey could not have been more different from the first. The first trip had gone smoothly, and the dogs had made the work seem easy. For the next trip, the men had decided they could add to the load. But they added too much, and the dogs could barely move the sledges. On top of that, their going was made more difficult by the thin layer of snow that had fallen and crusted on top of softer drifts below. As the thin veneer cracked underneath them, the dogs' paws became bloody and sore. The temperature, too, kept dropping, starting at 5°F but quickly going down to -20°F and then down to -40°F by early March. Even for the dogs, it was just too cold.

On the upside, the men breathed a sigh of relief every time they saw the dried fish, "which stood out sharply against the white snow and were very easy to see," Amundsen remembered.[92] Knowing how these markers eased their journey, Amundsen came up with another plan. At each depot, he decided, they would lay flags east and west—perpendicular to the intended north/south route—for five and a half miles in each direction. By numbering the flags, anyone would know

*Amundsen and his men traveled in a line of dogs pulling sledges,
with men skiing next to them. [Wikimedia Commons]*

where they were in relation to the depot. Fatigue, hunger, and snow
blindness could easily lead even the best men astray; they all knew
these markers might be the difference between life and death. They
laid their first set of flags out at the 80° depot and kept moving.

Again and again the men brought out the whips. The dogs were
emaciated, unable to keep up with the weight or the weather. Their
paws were cracked and raw. Yet still the men kept driving them.
Amundsen was adamant: "Our fight for the Pole was entirely dependent on this autumn work, in laying down large supplies of provisions
as far to the south as possible."[93] If they expected to survive the race
to the pole and back, they needed this food.

Eventually, though, it was pointless to go on. The dogs would die if they went farther. Amundsen decided to change the plan and set down their last depot at 82°, not 83°, sixty-nine miles short of his goal. They left 1,370 pounds of supplies (mostly dog food) and a sledge, piled a cairn twelve feet high, and raised a bamboo flagpole and flag even higher to mark the spot. As before, they laid numbered flags to the east and west. Then they turned home.

The men had planned on riding back comfortably in the sledges, but they quickly gave that up for the sake of the dogs. They skied alongside their companions, urging them on when they faltered, lifting them to their feet when they couldn't get up, gentle now that the depots had been laid. Still, despite their care, eight dogs perished on the return journey.

They made one more small trip that summer, using new, fresh dogs. Once more, the men returned to 80° south to drop off as much seal meat as they could carry. The meat would stay frozen; an all-you-can-eat stop for the dogs would be welcome when they raced to the pole.

When the men finally returned to camp, they were set for winter to close in. The jolly cook, Lindstrom, had made Framheim snug while the others were on the depot journeys. Amundsen "frankly confess[ed]" that "I have never lived so well" with hot food, work, happy dogs, and the ethereal glow of the Aurora Australis for inspiration in the long, dark polar night.[94] By the end of the winter, they were rested, fit, and well-fed.

All they needed was the sun.

*"As much as my solo crossing of Antarctica
with no outside assistance will be a test of my
physical endurance, even more so it will be a
true test of my mental strength."*

~Colin O'Brady, October 20, 2018 [95]

*"Staying focused and positive despite the inevitable
setbacks is key. With much still to do I continually
remind myself why I'm doing this, to honour the
legacy of the early polar pioneers, for Henry and for
the next generation of aspiring adventurers."*

~Lou Rudd, July 17, 2018 [96]

CHAPTER 6

THE SETUP,

O'BRADY/RUDD:
OCTOBER 2018

Punta Arenas, Chile—October 2018

If Lou had been a superstitious man, he might never have left England. The day before he boarded a plane for Chile, his wife underwent unexpected surgery. His twenty-one-year-old son couldn't get leave from the Royal Marines to say goodbye. At the airport, his two daughters, twenty-four and twenty-one years old, hugged him with tears streaming down their faces. It seemed like an inauspicious start.

He had been away from his family plenty of times in the past. But he had never gone alone. Would he have the strength? Henry had been only a few years older than Lou on his final journey. Lou promised his family that he would come back to them. But, then again, so had Henry.

Lou left England on October 26, 2018, bound for Punta Arenas, Chile. As one of the closest port cities to Antarctica, Punta Arenas was the final transition from civilization into the unknown. Bounded by the Strait of Magellan, brightly colored buildings and roofs almost glowed in a low skyline. Here, in one of the most southern cities in the world, Lou met with the company working to ensure his survival: Antarctic Logistics and Expeditions (ALE).

No one gets to the South Pole entirely alone. When Lou designed his route, it was ALE's experts that checked his plans and suggested improvements, using their detailed maps that showed the locations of crevasses and flow rates of the ice. If Lou became sick or injured,

Punta Arenas, Chile. [Oscaroyarzo/Wikimedia Commons]

it would be ALE's doctors that he would call, and it was ALE's rescue team that would attempt to reach him if the worst should happen, just as they had for Henry.

Lou flew down to Chile with Wendy Searle, his expedition manager. Wendy, a polar explorer herself planning a solo trip to the South Pole in 2020, had agreed to oversee his progress, keep track of the conditions of his route, and post daily updates to Lou's blog. Wendy explained that "whenever he's finished for the day, it'll be midnight in the UK so he'll ring up and leave a voicemail—just a normal voicemail—on my phone," which she would then transcribe for Lou's followers to read online.[97] It was a daily personal connection to life back home.

As soon as they arrived in Punta Arenas, Lou and Wendy went to work. Lou's pulk, food, fuel, and skis had been flown down via cargo planes ahead of him, and ALE had all of his gear waiting when he arrived. In a bright green warehouse with cement floors, brick walls, and metal pillars supporting the roof, Lou and Wendy checked over every piece of food and gear.

When he wasn't looking over his supplies, Lou met with doctors. He was in excellent health, but anything could happen on the ice. The best defense in an emergency was preparation. Steve Jones, the ALE Planning and Expeditions Manager, explained that the ALE doctors "needed a comprehensive list of absolutely everything in their medical kit." In an emergency, they wouldn't waste time asking, "Do you have this?" "Do you have that?"[98] In an emergency, the doctors would already know.

ALE mandated that everyone headed to Antarctica needed to be in Punta Arenas for five days before their scheduled flight to the continent. There were plenty of last-minute preparations to make, but even more so, Antarctica itself now dictated their schedule. The weather on the continent and the conditions there were unpredictable and changed rapidly. Steve Jones explained that they "reserve the right, if the weather's going to be terrible tomorrow, and we're all ready the evening before, let's fly the evening before."[99] Everyone who was headed to Antarctica had to be ready as soon as they had clearance.

Everyone.

It was inevitable that Lou and Colin would meet. It had been inevitable since the moment Colin announced his expedition. In a race to be the first, starting early was imperative, and there was only one way to get to the start.

They decided to see each other on their own terms, rather than leave it to fate. Over drinks at a basement bar in Punta Arenas, where the rocky foundations of the building above were exposed as walls, and pine paneling and porthole windows gave it a seaworthy feel, the two explorers finally came together.

It was uncomfortable, awkward. They were competitors, and they were wary of the other's strategy, of Lou's experience, and of Colin's youth and strength. They had their own reasons and motivations for going, but they had the same goal. They wouldn't have gone, if each didn't think he could be the first.

But the awkwardness didn't last for long. They were more alike than they were different. Few people ever go to Antarctica and even fewer ever pull a pulk. Only a handful ever travel solo. Only two other people, outside of the two who sat that night at a table at La Taberna, had ever attempted to travel solo, unaided, and unsupported across the continent. Lou and Colin could understand each other in a way almost no one else could. Their friendship was almost as inevitable as their meeting.

They compared routes and realized that they might cross paths. A smile, a word of encouragement, a wave in the middle of a vast, unbroken horizon would be something to look forward to. They would see each other again, that much was for certain.

They left that night, friendly if not actually friends, each to his own preparations. Antarctica was only days away.

Lou Rudd with his pulk and harness in Punta Arenas, Chile.
[TAMARA MERINO/New York Times/Redux]

In an Airbnb across town, Colin was making similar last-minute preparations as Lou. Colin's wife, Jenna, had come with him down to Chile, and she helped him with all of the final checks. Like Wendy, Jenna was Colin's expedition manager. Without Jenna's organization and planning "brilliance," Colin readily admitted, "this project would have remained just a dream."[100]

Outside of ALE, she would be his link to the rest of the world, though brief satellite calls and short texts or emails would be their

Penguins, not polar bears, live on the coast of Antarctica. [Jason Auch/Wikimedia Commons]

only way to communicate. For the moment, they would cherish their last days together, as they checked and rechecked all of his supplies.

Thankfully, the Colin Bars had made it to Chile. They were designed for the frigid temperatures of Antarctica, and the heat of travel had threatened to turn them into a gooey mess. The only way to get them to Punta Arenas had been to ship them in boxes of ice. Now, they were safely back with Colin, and he and Jenna divided each bar into small pieces. The bars were soft at room temperature, but at -20°F, Colin could easily break a tooth by trying to take a bite.

Amid planning and packing, Colin also regularly posted to Instagram and tweeted with students in classrooms around the world about the Impossible First expedition, as he was calling his journey. Promoting engagement and helping other people conquer their impossible goals was always part of his vision. When he started getting a lot of comments and questions about polar bears, he responded that "there are no living things at all in the interior of the Frozen Continent."[101] It was a harsh truth, knowing that "it will just be me and my thoughts out there alone on the ice," Colin wrote.[102] (In any case, polar bears only live in the Arctic, not the Antarctic.)

The call for departure came, at last, early on October 31, 2018. Weather had cleared, and the plane was ready. Antarctica was waiting.

Lou and Colin both boarded the Ilyushin-76TD jet with the ALE staff. The Ilyushin was a massive, four-engine, heavy-duty freighter with a 165-foot wingspan, capable of carrying an entire school bus, originally designed to be flown to the most isolated parts of

Siberia. The pilot and copilot flew the plane from the cockpit, but a disorienting bubble of windows stretched below the nose for a navigator to sit and guide the plane through the most remote areas on Earth.

For the four-and-a-half-hour flight, Colin and Lou sat on hard benches with the other ALE crew on the first jet flight of the season to Union Glacier, Antarctica. They landed on blue ice, a naturally occurring runway called a "skiway."[103] The plane stopped without any skidding or sliding; the ice was not slippery below 15°F.

They stepped onto Antarctica. The words were familiar—ice,

Ilyushin-76TD landing on blue ice runway in Antarctica. [Adam Ungar/ALE]

mountains, snow, sun—but the effect was paralyzing. It was their home for the next several months.

A skeleton ALE crew had arrived days before on a small, ski-equipped plane. Their job had been to move the buildings back into place. The Union Glacier camp was seasonal, entirely dismantled at the end of each January when the field of double-walled, clam-shelled tents that housed guests were taken down and stored for next season. More substantial structures that couldn't easily be flown off the continent were moved into the shelter of the mountain. If they had been kept in place all winter, they would've been buried in snowdrifts. Now, at the very beginning of the season, the early ALE crew had made certain that the buildings were ready, and everything essential was there.

"There's nothing," assured Steve Jones, "to delay [Colin and Lou's] departure."[104]

There was another flurry of activity for the two explorers. Just like in Punta Arenas, they once again checked over their supplies and met with doctors. They also met with the communications team and each signed up for a nightly call-in slot, carefully choosing a time when they expected to be in their tents.

ALE actively monitored each expedition out in the field. Every single expedition—scientists, explorers, or tourists—was given a ten-minute slot in which to call in every night. Every day, without fail, expeditions reported their location in latitude and longitude, their amount of time in the field, the distance they had traveled, and any problems—physical, mental, or technical—that they had encountered. Once a week, doctors took over the call and asked in-depth medical questions. Skipping the nightly call-in was not an option.

ALE Union Glacier base camp with rows of guest tents and a line of service buildings.
[Christopher Michel/ALE]

If for some reason an expedition missed the call, "it starts a clock ticking," said Steve Jones.[105] Though there were a series of other call numbers to try to reach ALE, a missed call triggered a twenty-four-hour countdown before ALE would issue additional responses. Forty-eight hours without contact meant deploying emergency search and rescue.

Aside from the nightly call-in, ALE also kept track of each expedition through GPS pings from tracking beacons and by monitoring their social media. "Everything they send out themselves on Twitter, Facebook, Instagram, their websites, their blogs, their voice recordings . . . those are all actively examined, not just monitored, and compared with what they've told us," Steve Jones said.[106]

Was there frostbite on a nose that someone had forgotten to mention? Did someone's gear look broken or in worse shape than they had reported? Was someone not owning up to a low mental state to ALE but admitting it to the rest of the world? It was all imperative for ALE to know. Survival and help might depend on it.

Lou and Colin were about to head into a great wilderness, at the very extreme of what humans could live through. Alone in their tents in Union Glacier, the men were determined that rescue and assistance would not be needed. They checked all their supplies—again. They met with doctors—again. They ate their last meals cooked in a kitchen and used the camp's phone to say their last goodbyes.

And then, it was done.

All that was left was to wait for the weather to clear.

And while they waited, the explorer and the athlete, they talked. Colin had a good idea, getting the elevation gain out of the way right at the start. But the weather . . . the weather would keep him in Union Glacier for weeks. And Lou's start at Hercules Inlet was geographically appropriate, but wouldn't the Messner Start put him on a more direct and shorter route to the pole? And, wouldn't it make more sense to compete head-to-head? The longer they talked and waited, the more an all-out race seemed to make sense.

There was one other big advantage of racing on the same course: sharing flights would save money. The flight between Union Glacier and the Leverett Glacier (or, between Leverett and Union Glaciers) cost $100,000. It was the most expensive part of the entire expedition. But, if they could share a flight, they could cut the price of a ticket in half.

Whether it came down to money or it came down to sportsman-ship, a change in route made sense. They talked it over and decided on a compromise: they would follow Lou's original direction but use Colin's start and ending points. It would be an all-out, first-to-the-finish competition.

The weather finally cleared on November 3, 2018. Just after noon, Lou and Colin boarded the ski-equipped Twin Otter plane and sat side-by-side for the ninety-minute, 265-mile flight from Union Glacier to the Messner Start. The plane touched down with skis skimming across the ice, making a runway for itself out of a plain of snow.

They dropped Colin off first. He hugged Lou—his last human con-tact until he reached the South Pole—and waved with both hands as the plane taxied one and a half miles down the ice shelf. Lou stepped out and gathered his pulk. Alone, with silence and an unbroken, white horizon cut into a clear, agonizingly blue sky, Antarctica stretched in front of him.

Privately, neither man thought they would both see the finish.

ANTARCTICA

----- INTERNATIONAL BOUNDARY

0   500   1000   Miles

0   500   1000   Kilometers

O C E

CIRCLE

ANTARCTIC

MARIE BYRD

EL

ROSS SEA

ROSS
ICE SHELF

DATE LINE

VICTORIA LAND

80

W ZEALAND

BALLENY
IS.

WILKES LAND

AUCKLAND
IS.

70

MACQUARIE I.

60

50

TASMANIA

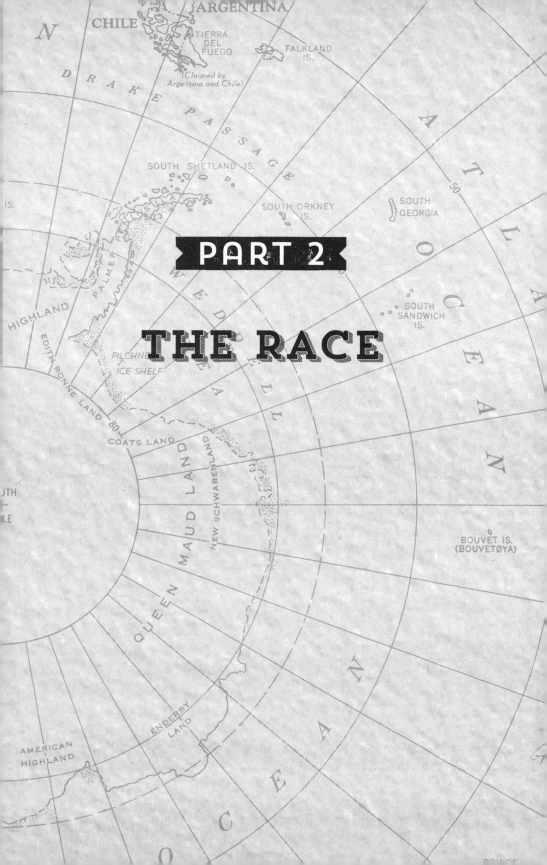

PART 2

THE RACE

"'We've been lucky,' said Wisting; 'this is the only place where the crevasse is narrow enough to put a sledge across. If we had gone a little more to the left . . . none of us would have escaped. There is no surface there; only a crust as thin as paper. It doesn't look very inviting down below, either; . . . immense spikes of ice sticking up everywhere, which would spit you before you got very far down.'"

~Roald Amundsen, October 21, 1911 [107]

"I write this sitting in our tent waiting for the fog to clear—an exasperating position as we are in the worst crevassed region. Teddy Evans and Atkinson were down [a crevasse] to the length of their harness this morning, and we have all been half-way down. As first man [in line] I get first chance [to fall], and it's decidedly exciting not knowing which step will give way."

~Captain Scott, December 21, 1911 [108]

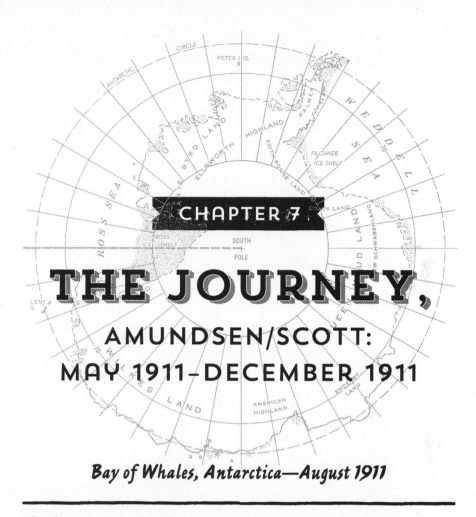

CHAPTER 7

THE JOURNEY,

AMUNDSEN/SCOTT:
MAY 1911–DECEMBER 1911

Bay of Whales, Antarctica—August 1911

The dogs were ready. The men were ready. The sleds were ready. Yet no matter how much Amundsen and his men paced around Framheim or shot stony glares at the sky, nothing would hurry the change of seasons.

Day by day, the men watched the thermometer: -60°F. -40°F. "At best," Amundsen admitted, "the climate in the Antarctic is about the worst in the world."[109]

There was nothing to do except wait and hope that Scott was suffering the same bad weather.

Then, on September 6, the thermometer read a heavenly -20°F. And

Over the course of the winter, the men at Framheim built tunnels and whole rooms for storage and extra work space into the Barrier snow. [Wikimedia Commons]

on September 7, it read a blissful -7°F! This was it, they thought. The break had come!

Amundsen had never been one for speeches. Before one of their trial runs, he had tried to think of something to say, feeling, as leader, he *ought* to say something. "I tried to work up a little poetry—'the ever-restless spirit of man'—'the mysterious, awe-inspiring wilderness of ice'—but it was no good," he wrote. "I abandoned my efforts, after coming to the conclusion that each sledge gave one more the idea of a coffin than of anything else, all the cases being painted black."[110]

In spite of Amundsen's silence, they raced off on September 8, less than a month after the summer sun first rose above the horizon. They left, dogs running, men shouting, the whole group flying over the ice.

But they had been too eager. Three days into their journey, the temperature fell to -68°F. And it stayed cold. The fluid in their compasses froze solid. By the time they turned back to Framheim, it was too late. Three dogs died. Two of the men were so frostbitten that their entire heels fell off—dead and rotting—in their boots.

It was too disappointing and too physically painful for some of them. Every group that has spent months cooped up together is bound to have conflict, and the false start shredded the peaceful veneer that had sheltered the group.

Amundsen decided, in one of his few outright commands, it was best not to all go on together. Carrying grudges to the pole could be deadly. Amundsen directed three of his men to explore land to the east. He would lead the remaining four to the pole.

And, again, they waited.

Men of Framheim sewing equipment for their coming journey. Amundsen is third from the right. [National Library of Norway]

This time, they stayed until they saw other signs of spring. The animals returned. Seals flopped up to the ice near Framheim. Antarctic petrels began flying above the camp. The sun was still weak, but Amundsen remembered with joy that "it was light—genuine daylight—and it was much appreciated."[111]

It was time, finally.

On October 19, 1911, Roald Amundsen, Olav Bjaaland, Helmer Hanssen, Sverre Hassel, and Oscar Wisting set off for the South Pole with fifty-two dogs and four sleds. They left without any fanfare. "Our coursers [dogs] were harnessed in a jiffy," he remembered, "and with a little nod—as much as to say, "See you to-morrow"—we were off."[112] The cook, the one remaining man at Framheim, did not even come out of the hut to say goodbye.

It was a job to hold the dogs back. The men were excited, eager, but the dogs were energy itself. Each dog driver had planned to walk behind the sledges, but the going was so easy and the dogs so enthusiastic that the men simply hopped on and enjoyed the ride. Amundsen was stunned: "We expected them to do well, but not so well as they did . . . We had never dreamed anything of the sort—driving on ski to the Pole!"[113] The dogs, the precious dogs, seemed made for the single purpose of flying over the Barrier ice.

By the time they reached 82°S, they had decided that the dogs needed to be forced to rest, to prevent them from burning out too early. From this point to the end of the Barrier, the men built cairns out of blocks of snow and ice every eight or nine miles. The point was to stop the dogs, but they all realized that the cairns might save a lost, weak team on the return. Amundsen was always trying to foresee how things could go wrong.

Yet even Amundsen couldn't predict what was to come. They had practiced traveling on the Barrier during the depot-laying missions. But what lay ahead, and what lay above them, had never been done. They had to find a way through the mountains, up to the polar plateau. The only known route up and over—Beardmore Glacier—was more than 250 miles away.

It was not only the distance, though, that prevented Amundsen from using Beardmore Glacier. Amundsen knew that Scott planned to follow Shackleton's route, and his sense of honor had long ago declared that "Scott's route was out of bounds."[114] They would just have to find another way.

By the time they stopped for the night on November 8, peaks had broken through the horizon. Nearer and nearer they drew to the mountain wall that separated Barrier from plateau.

The closer they came, the more rock they saw. Mountains far to the south were white. Mountains directly in front of them were white. But in the middle, "what struck us all," Amundsen remembered, "were the bare sides . . . we had expected to see them far more covered with snow."[115] Cliffs of rock were dark marks against the Antarctic landscape. Without snow, they couldn't pull the sledges, and no one knew if they would find a passable route.

They chose a line, trying to connect snow run to snow run, zigzagging their way around rocks and cliffs to finally reach a wide glacier, which they christened Axel Heiburg. They pushed on, trusting that their view from the Barrier proved a navigable route. If the men were nervous, it didn't show.

They began climbing on November 17. The dogs pushed forward bravely, traveling eleven and a half miles and ascending 2,000 feet in the first day alone.

Up and down they went, over and over, descending 800 feet one day

Dark, bare sides of mountains like these worried Amundsen and his men.
[Christopher Michel/ALΣ]

and ascending 1,250 feet the next. Ascents were difficult, but the descents were dangerous. On a long, steep slope, speed could easily get out of control. "If this should happen," Amundsen wrote, "there is a danger, not only of [the sledge] running over the dogs, but of colliding with the sledge in front and smashing it."[116]

They began wrapping ropes around the sled runners to act as a brake, winding thin cords just a few turns if the descent was slight or wrapping thick rope many times around if it looked to be steep. It all had to be done by guessing what lay ahead; they couldn't afford the time to send scouts.

Every foot they gained seemed to come at an incredible price. They doubled up the dogs, slowly, painfully clawing their way up each slope, using four full teams to pull just two of their four sledges. It was the only way up, even though the double teams had to return for the remaining two sledges and climb each slope again. Even the sections of flat plains were now filled with loose snow that made pulling hard. The dogs grew so hungry that they began gnawing at the wood of the sleds, even after eating a full pound of pemmican for dinner every night.

Inch by inch, they crawled toward the last big hill. The night before their final ascent to the plateau, avalanches thundered in an ominous sign. The next morning, November 20, 1911, eager to be done and through, they hitched single teams to the sledges and hoped the dogs would have the strength needed.

The dogs seemed to understand. Scraping and pulling with effort that left claw marks on the ice, they crested the final ridge. After traveling seventeen geographical miles with 5,750 feet of ascent—more than a mile of vertical climb—in just one day, they reached the polar plateau.

Yet, not a single person celebrated. It had long been planned that this camp at the height of the mountains would be named the Butcher's Shop. They had made their ascent, and they would not have to make it again. So many dogs were no longer needed for the journey forward. What was needed was meat.

Amundsen, the lone man without charge of a dog team, ran inside the tent as soon as it was raised. With loud pumps and bangs, he rushed to get the stove started. As water boiled, he threw ingredients into the pot and "was unusually industrious in stirring it," he remembered, so that the spoon clanged the sides.[117] His one-man cacophony was no competition for the sound when the first shot rang out across the plain.

"Twenty-four of our brave companions and faithful helpers were marked for death," Amundsen remembered. Each sled driver shot and butchered six of his own dogs, throwing the entrails to be hungrily torn to pieces by those left living. The meat was carved and frozen—for dogs and for men—to eat later.

"We had agreed to shrink from nothing in order to reach our goal," remembered Amundsen stoically, but "the holiday humour that ought to have prevailed in the tent that evening—our first on the plateau—did not make its appearance; there was depression and sadness in the air—we had grown so fond of our dogs."[118] Their sacrifice was necessary. It was food. It was life. But the men mourned.

In a few days, with rest and fresh meat, both men and dogs found they could continue on with renewed energy. Little hills and rises still lay ahead, but the toughest climbs were behind them. They were together and healthy. They had made it through the mountains and up to 10,920 feet above sea level. They had ascended to the plateau.

The pole was dead ahead.

Cape Evans, Antarctica—October 1911

For the whole long, cold winter, Captain Scott once again fought his darkness. A gloom had hung around him since returning from depot-laying with only two ponies. Of course he was happy all the men were safe, but the loss of the ponies was devastating. It was hard news made harder coming on the heels of discovering Amundsen in the Bay of Whales . . . a whole degree closer to the pole than Scott and his men!

It had been a risky move on Amundsen's part, and it was far from

Beardmore Glacier, the one known route to the polar plateau. But to have saved almost seventy miles . . . It was a blow to Scott, and a bad one.

All winter, Scott had planned and organized. The journey to the pole would be a complex series of logistics handled by four different modes of transportation. First, the motor sledges would leave Cape Evans with two engineers and two assistants. When the motor sledges inevitably broke down, the four men would continue to man-haul until the other teams caught up. Then, not before November 1 to ensure warm weather, the pony teams would leave, followed by the dog teams a few days later.

Of the sixty-five men aboard the *Terra Nova*, Scott would only take sixteen of them across the ice. But just who to take was not an easy

Scott's skis, using a boot/binding combination invented and improved by the ski instructor, Gran, while in Antarctica. [National Library of Norway]

question. Back and forth Scott went in his journal, recording how one or another of the men had surprised him with hard work while others fell out of favor. They did not know exactly what he was thinking, but every man knew that Scott spent the winter deciding their fate.

Some men held nothing back in their desire to shine. Cherry-Garrard and Bowers joined Dr. Wilson on a trip to gather penguin eggs in the dead middle of winter. The journey nearly killed them.

But, Scott was impressed. "[Bowers] is a positive treasure, absolutely trustworthy and prodigiously energetic," he wrote in his journal. And of his old friend, Dr. Wilson, he had nothing but the highest praise: "I believe he really is the finest character I ever met . . . whatever the matter, one knows [Dr. Wilson] will be sound, shrewdly practical, intensely loyal and quite unselfish."[119] All three were shoo-ins for the journey south.

A few weeks later, Teddy Evans and two others made another winter journey in the twilight of August to check on the Corner Camp depot. Scott thought their trip was only asking for needless suffering, but he let them go. And he added it to his notes.

For those who made the cut to begin heading south, the tryout had only begun. Along the way, Scott would send men home. Sixteen would leave Cape Evans, but only four—Scott and three others—would see the pole.

On September 13, Scott announced his plans. On October 24, 1911, the motor sledge party, Teddy Evans, Bernard Day, Frederick Hooper, and William Lashly, left Cape Evans. The motor sledges hauled for more than a week before the engines broke, and the four men began man-hauling 740 pounds of supplies on November 1.

By coincidence, Scott left Cape Evans with the ponies and nine other men, including Dr. Wilson, Bowers, Oates, Edgar Evans,

Bunks in Scott's Cape Evans hut (October 9, 1911). All five men would start on the journey to the pole less than a month after this picture was taken. Top row (left to right): Bowers, Oates, Meares. Bottom row: Cherry-Garrard and expedition doctor, Atkinson. [Herbert Ponting/Wikimedia Commons]

Cherry-Garrard, and Crean, that same date. They traveled by night, using the slight lowering of the sun to make traveling easier on the ponies. For the men, too, it was convenient for everything but eating. "I don't like these midnight lunches," Scott wrote, "but for man the march that follows is pleasant."[120]

They had only been traveling for a week when the dog teams, driven by Meares and Dimitri, reached them on November 7. The dogs had come up so fast! It had almost been too fast. If the dogs had left later, they wouldn't have eaten rations from the sledges.

The group moved slowly. Blizzards came fast and furious—and

Men exploring a grotto in an iceberg, with the Terra Nova in the background.
[Herbert Ponting/Wikimedia Commons]

frequently. "We could see little or nothing," Scott wrote one night, "and the driving snow hit us stingingly in the face."[121]

The ponies were miserable, just as they had been on the depot-laying trips the year before. Their longer coats had grown in, but the snow fell in fine particles that worked its way beneath their blankets, under their fine fur, and irritated their skin. "We men are snug and comfortable enough," Scott admitted, "but it is very evil to lie here and know that the weather is steadily sapping the strength of the beasts on which so much depends."[122]

Nothing much seemed to bother the dogs, though. With nictitating eyelids, a translucent membrane that could slide horizontally over each eye, the dogs could travel in even the hardest of driving snow. They were warm and snug and traveled easily on the ice.

But they all had to stay together, and the group could only go as fast as its slowest member.

Shackleton's weather had been fine! In the same place, in the same season and even month, he had clear skies. Scott had blizzards. Shackleton's ponies had traveled easily! Scott's ponies stumbled in the snow and winds.

All of Scott's plans were built around the reports handed down from Shackleton. He knew the only way to reach the pole and come back safely was to match or beat Shackleton's schedule.

After twenty-nine days of traveling, they were already six days behind Shackleton's position, and Shackleton's pace hadn't even gotten him to the pole. Scott had to be faster.

The ponies were doing their best, but for all of Oates's careful attention to the animals, he couldn't change the weather. The ponies sunk into the deep drifts, and the men had to dig them out every time they stopped to eat or sleep. It was a journey of hundreds of miles taken step by step.

And step by step, they found the ground was beginning to change. On December 3, Cherry-Garrard wrote that they "began to cross the great undulations in the Barrier, with crests some mile apart."[123] Up and down these waves, they marched on. And as they marched, the waves began to come closer and closer together. Within a few days, they were traveling across ridges twelve or fifteen feet high. As far as they could see, east and west, stretched "a great white line of

Captain Scott standing next to pressure ridges. [Herbert Ponting/Wikimedia Commons]

jagged edges, the chaos of pressure"—bottomless crevasses and giant sheets of vertical ice that made the route almost impassable: the
shear zone.[124] Formed when the glaciers flowing down the mountains
crashed into the Barrier ice over seawater, it was the most dangerous
terrain of the entire expedition.

Shackleton had found a way through. He had marked his path, going just west of a mammoth, inescapable crevasse. But there was no
hope of following his line in a blizzard. They needed one clear day.
Just one.

Then, impossibly, the weather worsened. The wind grew. The snow
fell relentlessly. Scott's journals are etched with misery: "Our case is
growing desperate. Evans and his man-haulers tried to pull a load
this afternoon. They managed to move a sledge with four people on
it, pulling in ski. Pulling on foot they sank to the knees. The snow all
about us is terribly deep. We tried [a pony] and he plunged to his belly
in it . . ."[125] They could barely move.

Then, the temperature rose, and the men hated the heat. On
December 8, Scott recorded that "the temperature remains +33°, and
everything is disgustingly wet."[126] Rivers of melted ice ran through
the tent, and the men's sleeping bags and boots grew heavy as the fur
absorbed the water. For four days they sat, unable to move forward,
eating into rations that had been marked for the hard journey on the
plateau.

When the weather finally broke, and the temperature once again
dropped below freezing, the men drove the ponies on. Turning first
one way and then another, evading crevasses and whipping the animals until they plodded on, they managed the last five miles to the
base of the entrance to Beardmore Glacier.

At this Shambles Camp, shots pierced the silence, one after another, as the men killed every remaining pony. Scott had planned that the dogs would continue for a few more days, but the ponies had gone as far as they could, and the men needed their meat. They pulled their triggers without hesitation, grateful that they need not drive the worn-out beasts any farther. Carefully, they packed the pony remains into the snow, keeping the meat to resupply them on the return journey.

On December 10, three sledges of man-hauling teams and two sledges of dog teams started up the long entrance ramp to Beardmore Glacier. Though it took an agonizing six hours to cover the last, steepest mile, they reached the glacier the next day and laid their Lower Glacier Depot that afternoon. The dogs, which had gone farther than anyone expected, turned back with Meares and his assistant, Dimitri, driving them.

For the first time, movement was entirely due to man power alone. Rather than curse the added load, they praised the purity of hauling. Dr. Wilson wrote in his journal, "Thank God . . . we begin the heavier work ourselves."[127]

Yet even their relief was no match for the horrible weather that seemed to follow them everywhere. In the deep, soft snow, the sledges capsized, toppling over as the snow brought one runner up higher than the other. "[T]he snow is worse than I have ever seen it . . . every step here one sinks to the knees and the uneven surface is obviously insufficient to support the sledges," Scott woefully recorded one night.[128] As the men fought to pull the sledges, their goggles fogged up with sweat, and they went snow-blind as they stared with naked eyes at the ice. Lips cracked and bled, faces blistered and scabbed from the sun. Man-hauling was a point of pride, but its toll was almost unbearable.

A Terra Nova *dog team taking a break next to a wall of ice.* [Library of Congress]

They laid a Mid Glacier Depot on December 17 and moved toward the center of the glacier, hoping to avoid the bottomless crevasses filled with sharp spears of ice that had plagued Shackleton's team. Scott drove the men relentlessly, hauling for eleven and twelve hours each day. The men all did what was asked of them, knowing that Scott was driving himself just as hard. Every night, he compared their location with Shackleton's. They were catching up.

For Scott, it was getting harder and harder to whittle down his final team. From the beginning, he had insisted that "there does not seem to be a single weak spot" in the men, calling them "good men and true."[129] Now, more than a month and a half into the brutal journey, the remaining men were all eager to continue on, and still Scott had to make cuts. He "dreaded the necessity of this choosing—nothing could be more heartrending."[130]

When Scott told Cherry-Garrard and three others that they were to turn back northward, the men were bitterly disappointed. The last day on Beardmore, they laid the Upper Glacier Depot, and the next morning, December 21, 1911, they splintered as the returning group headed back to Cape Evans.

Scott and seven men—Bowers, Crean, Teddy Evans, Edgar Evans, Lashly, Oates, and Dr. Wilson—moved forward. "We are struggling on, considering all things, against odds," Scott wrote in his journal.[131]

The most encouraging sign, and the one that kept all of their spirits up, was the clean snow. Everyone assumed the Norwegians would take the one, known route to the polar plateau: up the Beardmore Glacier. Scott's team had not seen any tracks from sleds, dogs, or men. Perhaps they were winning after all.

Scott and his men raced on, racing Amundsen and the Norwegian team, racing to beat Shackleton's pace, pushing themselves harder than ever day after day. Each man knew Scott had planned rations to take only one team to the pole, and every man thought the others were weaker. Though they were wasting away, consuming barely half the calories they were burning, not a man wanted to be sent back. The pole called to them all.

"Full of emotion, excitement and perhaps a little intimidated by the task at hand, I loaded up my sled, slipped on my harness and took my first steps South toward the Pole. 'A journey of a thousand miles begins with a single step . . .' A saying has never before been quite so apropos."

~Colin O'Brady, November 3, 2018 [132]

"To be finally at the start point was an incredible moment, and I owe so much to so many people, helping me to get to this point. So then I said farewell to the pilot and the plane taxied, and I just stood and watched it disappear into a little black speck in the distance. And then complete silence. It really was a deafening silence and it was really eerie."

~Lou Rudd, November 3, 2018 [133]

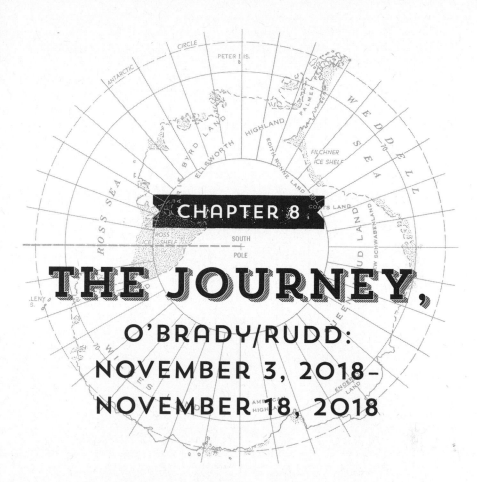

CHAPTER 8

THE JOURNEY,

O'BRADY/RUDD:
NOVEMBER 3, 2018–
NOVEMBER 18, 2018

Two miles north of the Messner Start, Antarctica—
Day 1—November 3, 2018

Lou was here. Finally. After so many months of planning and years of training, he could hardly believe it.

It was a bright, clear Antarctic day. He thrilled to be out once again on the ice, to face what lay in front of him, to walk out and test himself against the unknown.

And yet there was a shadow over the start—a six-foot-tall American shadow.

Of course Lou wanted to win. It *should* be a British explorer who made the journey first; they had already made two attempts. But Lou knew his goal, and he held to it: finishing, making it to the end and honoring Henry, was more important than winning. Getting pulled into a race mentality would only lead to burnout, the injury-inducing exhaustion that felled expeditions that started too hard and too fast.

Lou had firm instructions for his team: "Don't tell me anything about Colin unless I ask."[134] He and the American had different strategies; he didn't want to second-guess his own decisions based on what Colin was doing and where he was. Lou trusted his experience. After all, Lou had been serving in the military for as long as Colin had been alive. A race was aggravating but immaterial. He was already going as fast as he could.

It was time to get moving.

The pulk sitting on the ice in front of him was the biggest he had ever pulled. The carbon-Kevlar sled was 7.5 feet long. Empty, it weighed 16.5 pounds. Full, on that first day, it weighed 364.

It was ridiculously heavy, and the unfortunate conditions on the ground made it feel heavier still. As luck would have it, 2018 was a year of bad snow—deeper powder than anyone had expected—a harsh El Niño season. Any other year, the pulk would have slid easily over ice, but this year, there was no escaping the crunch of snow as the pulk sank several inches. Every step forward, Lou would have to pull against the resistance of snow as well as the weight of the pulk.

On top of that, the entire way to the South Pole was uphill. The uninterrupted horizon gave him no reference point—it was impossible to see that the ground was sloped up. But Lou could feel it.

Lou gritted his teeth and laid into his harness. "Really tough going," Lou posted in his first blog entry.[135]

He refused to even think about the possibility of giving up. Everything he would miss about home, all the little luxuries like daily showers, fresh food, clean underwear, and indoor plumbing, he boxed it all up in his mind and put it at the finish line. His plan was simple. "The only way you're ever going to get any of that back—your old life, everything you know and love—is by skiing,"[136] he told himself. The only way back to those things he craved was to finish.

That first day, in five hours of hauling, Lou skied a measly four and a half miles.

It was easy to be frustrated with the low mileage, with the outsized pain from such a short distance. It was hard to believe that the pulk would get lighter as he ate through food and hard to remember that his body would sink into a routine of hauling. So much of the expedition was a mental battle.

But Lou had a lifetime of resilience to rely on. He had lived through worse. In Antarctica, no matter how hard it got, at least no one was shooting at him. And, he got to sleep in a tent *all night*. On military duty in Norway, he had to wake up at "3:00 am to lay outside the tent on sentry duty," Lou remembered. Compared to that, this expedition was "just cold-weather camping."[137] He had made it through plenty of hard times before.

When Lou woke up the next morning, Day 2, Colin was behind him by about an hour's worth of hauling, "a bit of a speck in the distance."[138] As Lou put in his hours for his first full day, Colin sank back into the horizon.

The second day was just as hard as the first. He fought to stay positive, focusing on how "things can only get better as the pulk gets lighter" as he ate through food.[139] The second day, in seven and a half hours of hauling, he managed to cover nine and a half miles. Rather than comparing that distance to the long-mileage days he had on other expeditions, he celebrated what he had been able to accomplish. It was all a matter of attitude.

Already, on only his second day out, Lou faced one of the greatest challenges to Antarctic travel: sastrugi. These were sharp waves, etched into the ice by the fierce wind blowing down the continent from the South Pole. These "speed bumps," sometimes three or four feet high, brought the pulk to a jarring halt, and Lou was forced to

Sastrugi, or ice ridges cut into the snow by the wind. Sometimes several feet high, they make traveling difficult for any Antarctic team. [NOAA Photo Library/Wikimedia Commons]

" . . . jerk forward with my hips and try and unblock it and then get the [pulk] moving again and it was a constant battle really all day . . ."[140]

Fighting with the sastrugi was difficult in good weather. In the best conditions, judging the height and depth of sastrugi against the brilliant white of snow was difficult. But in spindrift, where the wind whipped up ground snow and enveloped Lou in a cloud of white as he hauled, the ridges seemed to blend seamlessly into flat ground. Over and over, he fell: "flat on my back laughing at myself completely in the middle of nowhere."[141] Laughing was far better than crying.

With his headphones alternating between 80s music and audio-books, Lou kept going forward. On clear days, he steered by setting a course, noting the angle of his shadow, and following it all day. In whiteouts, he stared at the compass strapped to his chest. Either way, he put one foot in front of the other and kept making progress.

Two miles north of the Messner Start, Antarctica— Day 1—November 3, 2018

Things began to go wrong for Colin as soon as he landed at the start.

As the ALE plane receded into the distance, Colin started loading his bags onto the pulk. He had checked, one by one, to make sure when the plane dropped him off that he had everything with him. Now, he loaded it all onto the pulk once more, securing the entire load and tightening straps across its belly.

Then with a slight "thwack," a strap broke.

It was just a strap. The remaining three would hold the load. His journey would go on.

But his gear was breaking, and he hadn't taken a single step forward.

When he finally did move, it was agony. He called Jenna in tears, using precious, expensive minutes on his satellite phone. "Maybe we didn't get it right," he cried to her.[142] His pulk was forty pounds heavier than Lou's. The veteran had taken off into the distance. To Colin, it looked like Lou was skiing on effortlessly. With all of his might, Colin could barely make the pulk budge.

Jenna was calm. Small steps would add up. "Just get to the start," she urged, telling him to haul just two miles his first day. "Set up your tent. You'll feel better."[143]

To make the race fair for both Colin and Lou, and to separate them so they weren't skiing side-by-side, the plane had dropped them one and a half miles apart, each two miles north of the official start. That first day, Colin's whole goal was to reach the marker between the glacier and the ice shelf—the Messner Start. For hours and hours, he trudged on, fighting for each step.

Back in Portland, Oregon, when he'd been training for the expedition, Colin sought advice from an expert polar explorer, Dixie Dansercoer. One of the most important things Dixie taught him was how to walk in a harness. Normal gait would only jerk the pulk; Colin needed "to walk like a duck," Dixie said, "sink a little deeper with the quads, like a human shock absorber."[144] It was an odd sort of waddling, but inch by inch, Colin struggled forward.

He made it to the marker that night, but it had used everything he had, mentally and physically, to get there. His distance for the first day was two miles. The end was more than nine hundred miles away.

On Instagram, he kept up a brave face, not describing the pain he'd endured, but admitting he was "perhaps a little bit intimidated by the task at hand."[145] To the outside world, he was simply excited to finally begin his Impossible First journey.

But in his tent that night, he called Jenna again. Fear, frustration, despair clouded his voice. "Tomorrow," she said, still remaining calm, "try to find the flow. Even if just for thirty seconds. Even if just for a minute. Just try to find that inner peace."[146]

The flow. Mental-physical interaction, how the brain and body responded to each other, had interested Colin for a long time. Certainly, his mind had overcome his burn injury in Thailand as much as his body. Ever since, he had chased flow states, where his mind and body worked seamlessly together, giving the perception of effortless athleticism. It was another goal, another prize to win along the way, rather than just eking out hard-won miles. Perhaps he would not travel far, but he could try to find the flow.

"We are the stories we tell ourselves," Colin often said, and he believed it with every part of his being. The morning of Day 2, Colin's first full day pulling a pulk, a mantra came to him. The same one he used during the Explorers Grand Slam when things got rough: "Colin, you are strong. You are capable."[147]

He said it out loud, repeating it. He said it until he believed it.

Lou was long gone in front of him, and Colin fought failure with every inch of forward progress, hour after hour, slow step by slow step.

Then, nine hours into the day, he found, for one single, breathtaking minute, a peace. Calm descended, and his mind and body united in fluent exertion. Colin found the flow.

In the next minute, it was gone, and the desperate reality of isolation and weight pulled him back under again.

But he had found it. For one minute. It was enough. He was

determined to go on and find that flow again. It was out there, on the journey in front of him, if only he could "calm my mind."[148]

It was overwhelming—an expedition of hundreds of miles, pulling hundreds of pounds behind him through deep snow. It was too big to face; even a full day of twelve hours of hauling was too daunting to think about. He broke the day into increments, a break every 90 minutes. Some water and a piece of a Colin Bar. Then back to hauling for another 90 minutes.

ALE's ski-equipped Twin Otter plane flying over Antarctica. [Bryan and Cherry Alexander/ALE]

At the end of the day, he had a regular routine: put up his tent, eat warm food, call ALE, and then call Jenna. The next day, he did it all again. One foot, however slowly, in front of the other. Each little bit added up.

It wasn't easy. He cried into his goggles on each of the first three days; the sheer difficulty of pulling the pulk made failure seem inevitable. His mind kept racing over all the ways things could go wrong. He had to be "like an airplane pilot," he later remembered, "with a constant checklist of this safety check: How are your feet? How are your hands? Is your nose okay? How are your feet? How are your hands?"[149] Over and over again, continually making sure nothing and no part of him was on the brink of failure. It was dull and relentless, and it was the difference between life and death.

But he kept going, and he kept giving himself messages of strength and quiet.

It was working. Colin was catching up.

At the end of the fifth day, Colin saw Lou's tent on the horizon.

It had been a long day. He had been up at 6:10 a.m., like he was every day. By 8:30 a.m., he was on his skis. But it wasn't until the very end of the day, after his usual twelve hours of hauling, that he saw Lou's tent in the distance. Instead of stopping, Colin kept going until he was a scant fifteen-minute ski away from the veteran.

The next morning, Colin woke up even earlier than usual. Whiteout. Snow flew in all directions as the wind whipped furiously around him. In Antarctica, whiteouts happened so often that they were no excuse not to haul, and Colin headed out into the unknown.

It happened quickly. Colin had barely skied for a few minutes that morning before he drew close to Lou's tent. The first change was a noise—a cough that wasn't his. It broke through the powerful rush of wind and the scrape of the pulk against the snow. Then, the sound of a zipper being undone.

It had been almost a week since the last time he saw someone, anyone, else. In the middle of the white blankness, Lou emerged from his tent and gave Colin a slow wave as he skied by.

Soon, Lou pulled alongside him on his own skis, having quickly dismantled his camp and loaded his pulk. It was early, and the conditions were awful. Still, Lou smiled and offered a hearty "Hey, good morning, mate!"[150]

Lou had noticed that Colin's harness looked off, like it was twisted somehow, and he started to ask if Colin needed—

Colin cut him off. His harness was fine; he knew about the twisting. That was just how he used his equipment.

Conversations like this couldn't happen. The stakes were too high. They were each fighting to capture a "solo" title; even a friendly greeting was too risky for Colin.

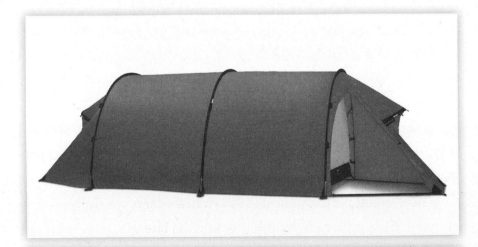

Both Colin and Lou used this three-person tent for their entire expedition. Anything that was wet and needed to dry overnight—clothes or even skis—would spend the night inside with them. [Hilleberg the Tentmaker]

Colin turned to face him. "Lou, let this be the last time we speak to one another."[151]

Lou raised his goggles and looked at the younger man. He nodded. Alone, unaided by even the momentary company of another person. The way it was meant to be.

They pulled apart and spent the rest of the day trading leads on parallel paths about a half mile apart, with visibility barely that far throughout most of the day. At the end of it, when Lou put up his tent, Colin skied on.

The next morning, Colin was up early once more. He left, into whiteout conditions again that made him feel like he was "inside a Ping-Pong ball."[152] Colin skied on as Lou slept, the distance between them growing the farther Colin went.

Colin traveled mostly in silence. As he let his mind wander and expand, he remembered stories and scenes that he thought he had forgotten long ago. Little moments, like swimming races from when he was five years old or car rides with his sister in high school, that normally seemed inconsequential came back to him as if he was "viscerally connected to the memory in all its vivid detail" during his hours of pulling his pulk, fighting his way across the Antarctic whiteout.[153]

It was these moments, these states of flow where his body, Antarctica, and his pulk seemed connected, that Colin lived for. He refused to be distracted by anything as mundane as excess noise, much less the pain of pulling the pulk.

Still, it was never truly silent in Antarctica—there were always the runners of the pulk against the snow and the bite of his skis cutting into the ice. But, even when they weren't moving, Antarctica provided its own accompaniment: the wind.

Rushing down the slope from the South Pole to the sea, katabatic winds charged headlong into the men. Some days it was little more than a stiff breeze, but, on the windiest days, the wind chill dropped the temperature from -4°F to a miserable -112°F. Back home in Oregon, a drop of 108° was the difference between sweltering while at the beach and needing thick mittens, warm boots, a coat, and a hat just to be outside; in Antarctica, the change was just as dramatic. Wind could make the cold feel so much colder.

On other days, fresh snow and spindrift ended his world mere feet in front of his face. He wrote home in messages that Jenna posted on Instagram: "When the weather is this poor, I literally have to stare at my compass on my chest mount all day long, keeping the compass needle pointed in the right direction. Sounds silly, but try closing your eyes and then try and walk in a straight line. It's nearly impossible. Without the compass to guide me, I'd basically be wandering around with my eyes closed. It's white in every direction."[154]

Yet even blinded, Colin was increasing his mileage. Fourteen- and sixteen-mile days were now his norm. One remarkable day, he even made twenty miles. He was strong. He was capable. He kept moving.

Then, on Day 14, Colin stopped. In the middle of a field of ice, just like the other fields of ice on the other days, with no visible marker showing any sign of importance, Colin raised his arms and cheered. He had made it to the first waypoint, the first navigation landmark.

Almost two hundred miles into the journey, he had reached a latitude and longitude marked on his GPS. That was it. No sign, no shelter of any kind. But he had made it.

He made a turn 30° west, set his compass on a new heading, and kept moving.

S

Antarctica—Day 7—November 9, 2018

Lou woke up the morning after Colin had passed him and saw no sign of the American. It was better that way. The long days of hauling were hard enough without constantly looking over his shoulder. It was a long, long race—anything could happen.

Not that Lou would be able to see Colin, even if they had been standing right next to each other. The wind was almost fully in his face, kicking up the spindrift that stung him as soon as he looked up. His face mask froze in place moments after he started. He had to be

The communications building at Union Glacier. Colin and Lou had nightly phone calls with ALE and once a week spoke with a doctor. [Christian Iversen/ALE]

quick to get it shaped right, or else he was forced to spend the day with uncomfortable bumps and ridges poking at him. It was a case of "head down, audiobook on, into the wind and just trudge away."[155]

By fate or coincidence, the worst weather yet came on the eve of Remembrance Day, the English version of Memorial Day. Lou had lost many friends to the horrors of war. He battled the wind, the snow, the loneliness, and fatigue, but the thought of friends who had perished in true violence spurred him on.

The next day, he rolled up his first large bag of food—ten days were done. All that weight. Gone.

He found a rhythm to his days, but that didn't mean hauling got any easier. The ground had still not turned icy as hoped, and the deep snow made it difficult to pull the pulk. The wind blew just off to the side of a headwind. Rather than offer any relief, this angle pushed against the pulk and "that's again adding to the resistance and it just felt like it [the pulk] weighed an absolute tonne," Lou wrote.[156] On the coldest days, adding even the heaviest layers—his fur ruff on his hood pulled tight around goggles and a face mask, multiple pairs of gloves inside windbreaks, called pogies, on the top of his ski sticks—didn't seem to dim the bite of freezing air.

Night offered no relief for his weariness. Lou was unable to sleep, kept awake by the idea that the wind might rip the tent apart. When the winds were at their worst, Lou would rouse himself once an hour to check the tent poles, making sure that they weren't about to snap from the strain. If it was very bad, he would go out and add piles of snow around the perimeter of his tent. Anything to help weigh down the edges and keep the tent from flying away.

Going outside made for a horrible night's sleep, but, even at midnight, the landscape outside his tent wasn't much different than during the day. Night, after all, didn't mean darkness in the polar summer. He could see perfectly well in sunlight that never waned.

Sound sleep or sleepless nights, it didn't matter. He kept marching on. The first turn, the first waypoint, didn't even merit a note in his blog when he passed it on Day 16. It was just a spot on the ice, and he had hundreds and hundreds of miles to go.

"It looked as if a battle had been fought here, and the ammunition had been great blocks of ice. They lay pell-mell, one on the top of another, in all directions, and evoked a picture of violent confusion. Thank God we were not here while this was going on, I thought to myself, as I stood looking out over this battlefield; it must have been a spectacle like doomsday, and not on a small scale either."

~ Roald Amundsen, November 28, 1911 [157]

"I never had such pulling; all the time the sledge rasps and creaks. We have covered 6 miles, but at fearful cost to ourselves."

~ Captain Scott, January 11, 1912 [158]

CHAPTER 9

THE POLE,

AMUNDSEN/SCOTT: NOVEMBER 1911– FEBRUARY 1912

Top of Axel Heiburg Glacier, Antarctica—November 23, 1911

Death was inescapable at the Butcher's Shop. Twenty-four dogs had been slaughtered, but those left living grew sleek once again, and hunger vanished from their eyes as they feasted on fresh meat. Amundsen and his men ate, too, and rested. Everyone regained their strength. But the place was forever marked with death in their minds—their renewed energy had come at a great price.

They stayed, bound to their tents by blizzards, for four days. Finally, unable to take the strain of boredom and death that haunted the camp, they unanimously voted to forge on in the middle of the

Axel Heiburg Glacier. [Jim Waldron/Wikimedia Commons]

storm. "Amid joking and chaff, everything was packed, and then—out into the blizzard," Amundsen wrote.[159] As they left camp, almost as an afterthought, Wisting stuck a broken ski into the snow as a marker for their supplies and cache of frozen dog meat.

It was nearly impossible for the men to keep their eyes open. Fine, abrasive particles of the driest snow pelted them as the wind drove everything wild in the storm. The dog drivers could not even see to the end of their team. Slowly, they kept on. Anything to get away from the Butcher's Shop.

For weeks, fog chased blizzard that chased fog. At one point, the air cleared slightly, and the men looked up with wonder at a mountain towering almost immediately over them. Amundsen quickly named it Mount Helland Hansen after a professor of oceanography back in Norway. Barely had he got the christening words out of his mouth before the peak slid back behind the gray curtain.

They slept lightly at night, ready to jump up at the first sign of sunlight. When light broke through the haze, they leaped out of their sleeping bags and raced outside to look around at their surroundings. While they could see, they chose a direction for the next morning's travel before heading back to bed. The weather had invariably turned again by the time they woke up a few hours later. They were the first people ever—ever—to see this part of Earth, and all they could describe was the gray, dense mist that clouded their entire view.

It was frustrating, and it was about to become dangerous. A few days out from the Butcher's Shop, their whole path became littered with crevasses that were "pale blue at the top, but end[ing] in the deepest black," Amundsen wrote.[160] The men roped themselves together. If someone fell, his only hope was whatever or whomever was at the other end of the rope. Perhaps the other man could be an anchor and stop his fall. Perhaps the rope would not snap under the dynamic load. Then again, perhaps not.

Between the crevasses, giant wedges of ice as big as a house with sides as sheer as a cliff called hummocks blocked their path. "Chasm after chasm, hummock after hummock . . . at last we found [a passage], if, indeed it deserved the name of a passage. It was a bridge so narrow that it scarcely allowed room for the width of the sledge; a fearful abyss on each side," wrote Amundsen.[161]

They named this plain the Devil's Ballroom and spoke in hushed voices of the terrible forces that must have wracked the earth to create this wasteland. Keeping a directly southern path was impossible as they wound their way around each obstacle. It took the men eight fraught days to escape this terrain.

At 11,070 feet—more than two miles—above sea level, the men gasped for air. At such a high altitude, even the simplest of acts left them winded. Amundsen wrote that "when I wanted to turn round in my [sleeping] bag, I had to do it a bit at a time, so as not to get out of breath."[162] Altitude sickness like Shackleton's headaches and nauseas hadn't appeared—yet—but they knew it was just a matter of time.

Despite the altitude, the three teams of six dogs managed whatever terrain they came across. But their hunger was growing. Every night when they stopped, the men had to hide all the leather, even to the point of burying the sleds in snow so the dogs wouldn't eat the lashings. Yet even as hungry as they were, the dogs did their job.

The worry now was the sun. Or, rather, the lack of the sun. As the lead dog driver, Hanssen had been navigating using dead reckoning, directing their course based on compass direction and distance traveled. It was a good approximation of where they were, but getting *approximately* to the South Pole would not make a record. They needed proof—data—to show they had reached the actual pole. They needed the sun.

Location—latitude and longitude—could be determined using a sextant, an accurate clock, and a set of navigational tables, but only if they could see the sun. For centuries, navigators had looked through a sextant, adjusting mirrors so that images of the sun at its highest point and the distant horizon came to appear on top of one another. Using the angle measured by the mirrors, and knowing the exact time the sun reached its highest point, anyone, anywhere in the world, could calculate their position with accuracy. Amundsen needed these hard numbers, these degrees, times, latitudes and longitudes, to prove that he had made it to the very bottom of the earth.

If only the fog would lift! They kept on, and their sledge-meters kept clicking away, noting the distance they traveled. They were getting close.

They stopped at 11:00 a.m. on December 7. Amundsen stood, staring at the sky, praying, wishing, hoping, trying with every fiber of his worn, determined body to drag the sun from the clouds.

And then, "whether my pulling helped it or not," said Amundsen, the sky began to clear. Moment by moment as it approached noon, the sun became more visible through the gray mist as "the curtain [of fog] was rent more and more," wrote Amundsen. "The feeling was something like that one has on waking from a good nap, rubbing one's eyes and looking around. We had become so accustomed to the grey twilight that this positively dazzled us."[163]

Quickly, before the sun could disappear, each man took out his sextant and adjusted the mirrors. They did the math. One after another, they looked up. Every answer matched:

A sextant. The eyepiece is at the top right, and the mirrors are directly opposite on the left.
[Andres Rueda/Wikimedia Commons]

88°16' south.

Eighteen miles past Shackleton's record! They were farther south than any man had ever been.

With the sun still shining, they started forward once again. Amundsen led the way, taking his turn as front man leading the dogs. Then, a great sound made him turn around. A cheer—a "jubilant shout"—pierced the Antarctic silence as the men celebrated being the farthest south.[164]

"All the sledges had stopped, and from the foremost of them the Norwegian flag was flying. It shook itself out, waved and flapped so that the silk rustled. . . . No other moment of the whole trip affected me like this."[165] Tears rolled from Amundsen's face as he turned around and went to shake hands with the only other people at the far reaches of the earth.

They laid a depot on December 8 at 88°25', shedding as much weight as possible from the sleds. Once again they began to build beacons, small three-foot-high cairns every two miles. The plain was flat and featureless. No signs of sastrugi. No crevasses. No blizzards. No ice ridges.

One hundred and nine miles to go to the pole.

December 9. December 10. The weather held, cold and clear. They were traveling nearly twenty miles per day.

December 11. December 12. The dogs began scenting. One, and then another, started sniffing due south. As though they were chasing *someone's* trail.

It wasn't possible, was it, that Scott had beaten them? They had made such good time. They had traveled in all kinds of weather and had barely slacked their pace. But why, without anyone else around, would the dogs keep trying to scent the way to the pole?

December 13. They camped mere miles away from their goal.

The only sounds came from their own men and dogs. The only tracks were of their own making. "It was like the eve of some great festival that night in the tent. One could feel that a great event was at hand," Amundsen said.[166]

December 14. Their necks seemed to grow extra inches as they craned to see farther ahead. "Not much was said, but eyes were used all the more," Amundsen wrote.[167]

Then, at 3:00 p.m.—in the middle of "a vast plain of the same character in every direction, mile after mile," Amundsen wrote[168]—the three dog drivers watching the sledge-meters shouted as if with one voice:

"Halt!"[169]

*"Poleheim"—home of the South Pole. Amundsen, Hanssen, Hassel, and Wisting (left to right)
face their tent with the Norwegian flag at the South Pole (Bjaaland was also present,
taking the picture). [Olav Bjaaland/Wikimedia Commons]*

They had reached the South Pole, and there was no sign of anyone else.

Into the snow, five pairs of hands raised the Norwegian flag, proud, independent, as the first mark at the bottom of the earth.

Amundsen, Hanssen, Wisting, Hassel, and Bjaaland—they had done it. They had made it to the South Pole!

It had been because of the dogs. It was their strength that had enabled the men, and they cherished their "best friends," as Amundsen put it.[170] The dogs and men—a team, together.

That night, the men celebrated with a bit of seal meat each and began marking "South Pole, December 14, 1911" on all their gear to serve as souvenirs later on.[171] A bigger party would have to wait until their return to Framheim—for now, there was still work to be done.

Amundsen was determined that their claim to the pole would be absolute. Their camp was close, but it was almost certainly not at the absolute pole—they had been traveling using imprecise dead reckoning since passing Shackleton's farthest south. Now they began to take hourly sextant readings, but, just to be sure of their claim, Bjaaland, Wisting, and Hassel skied twelve and a half miles in three different directions away from the camp: east, south, and west. The pole certainly lay within the box bounded by their short journey.

On their third day of their camp at Poleheim, home of the pole, Amundsen decided to send two men out once more. Bjaaland and Hanssen, on a course suggested by their hourly sextant readings, skied four miles away from camp and likely reached within meters of the true pole.

They had done what they needed to do, and they had stayed as long as they dared. It was time to go home.

Just before they left, they raised a spare tent as the one monument they would leave behind. As they unfurled it, they found messages from the crew sailing the *Fram*, who knew Amundsen planned to use the tent in victory. "Good luck" and "Welcome to 90°" warmed them as only the voices of distant friends could.[172]

There wasn't much the men could leave behind, but they gave what they could, knowing someone else might need it much more: a sextant, a case for an instrument to measure altitude, three reindeer-skin boots, and a few mittens. Amundsen also left two letters: one to King Haakon of Norway and the other to Captain Scott. Anything might happen on the way back, and these letters would serve as his record.

Three days after they had first arrived, they left, following their old tracks, looking over their shoulders every few minutes. Not one of them would ever return to the pole again.

S

Polar plateau, Antarctica—December 31, 1911

Just 100 miles to the east, a very different group was headed in the opposite direction. On the last day of 1911, Amundsen and Scott passed each other at 87°S, the blank horizon concealing the other's path. Not knowing that the Norwegians had already turned homeward, Scott and his remaining seven men trudged southward. They still had not seen any tracks from Amundsen, and their hopes rode high. Only 180 miles stood between them and the pole.

But a lot can occur in 180 miles. And when danger strikes, it can happen in an instant.

Like the moment when Edgar Evans slit his hand. He had practiced

Dog team from the Terra Nova *expedition. All hauling on the polar plateau, and most on Beardmore Glacier, was done by men. [Herbert Ponting/Wikimedia Commons]*

remaking the twelve-foot-long sledges into ten-foot-long versions before, but never at this altitude and never at these temperatures. He slipped, and his hand bled. Quickly, he stuffed his fist into his glove, and no one else was any wiser. In his journal, Scott noted that "the job of rebuilding [the sledges] is taking longer than I expected," but there was no other sign that anything was wrong.[173] Edgar Evans kept notice of his wound well away from Scott. Any injury, he knew, would be grounds for elimination from the polar team.

There was still one more cut to make. Scott had planned to take only three others with him to the pole. Half the team would not continue on. But just who that would be, no one knew.

It was easy for the men to guess that Teddy Evans and Lashly would not be chosen. They had been man-hauling for four hundred miles since the motor sledges broke back on the Barrier, and they were worn through. Even they were surprised that they had not been sent back to Cape Evans before.

But who else?

Dr. Wilson was Scott's closest friend and a strong hauler. Bowers, too, had proven his worth as a hauler and time-and-again purveyor of indestructible good luck. It was a good guess that both would keep going south.

The remaining three—Crean, Edgar Evans, and Oates—were almost a toss-up. Two would have to turn around.

Or, Scott began to think, was that the wisest choice? A formation of five men, not four, could easily be formed to haul the sledge. A bit of extra weight in food and fuel would be added to the sledge, but that would be more than made up for in terms of added power. Speed, more than anything, seemed to matter most.

Scott made up his mind. On January 3, 1912, he told Crean, Teddy Evans, and Lashly they would be the last team to leave. Scott decided that *both* Edgar Evans and Oates had the power and strength to help them as a five-person team to the pole.

Crean and Lashly were both horribly disappointed, and Scott wrote that "poor old Crean wept" when he was told he would not see the pole.[174] When they turned around, Crean, Lashly, and Teddy Evans carried final instructions for those waiting at Cape Evans: bring the dog teams with extra supplies and meet Scott between 82° and 83°S in the middle of February.

For the ones chosen to go to the pole, Dr. Wilson wrote as if he spoke for all of them: "I am one of the five to go on to the Pole . . . It seems too good to be true . . ."[175]

Scott had made his decision, and he could not change his mind. The five men were bound together for the rest of their journey.

Yet Edgar Evans was not the only one hiding an injury from Scott. In his journal, Oates spent day after day writing about pain radiating from his ankle. But his complaint didn't go farther than the pages in his book; Oates told no one and was careful to keep his injury hidden.

Only a few days later, Edgar Evans couldn't keep his own wound a secret. His knuckle was swollen with pus, and Dr. Wilson drained it while waiting for a blizzard to die down on January 8. It was too late to send the injured man back to Cape Evans; he would never survive the journey alone. The only option was to keep pressing forward, praying that his injury did not grow worse.

The very next day, January 9, they passed 88°S, Shackleton's farthest south. "RECORD," Scott wrote at the top of his journal entry that night, celebrating with the only means he had.[176]

It was good news, but the drudgery, the cold, and the weight of the sledge were inescapable. "I found to my horror we could scarcely move the sledge . . . towards the latter end of our tiring march we began to make better progress, but the work is still awfully heavy," wrote Scott on January 10.[177] They began passing through waves of depression and homesickness. They stayed hopeful of their chances to win against Amundsen—they still hadn't seen any other tracks in the snow—but optimism was becoming hard to hold.

Scabs from the wind and sunlight covered every bit of exposed skin, and their lips were cracked, bloody messes. They struggled with sastrugi almost every day.

Scott claimed that they were all feeling very strong, but that was almost an outright lie. Edgar Evans's hand showed no signs of healing. In the thin atmosphere, with an insufficient diet, his knuckle was horribly disfigured, no matter how many times Dr. Wilson bandaged it. Though Oates still had not confessed to his injured leg, Scott had already noted in his journal that "Oates seems to be feeling the cold and fatigue more than the rest of us . . ."[178] The men were far from healthy, and Scott walked a fine line between optimism and outright blindness.

Temperatures began falling. The end of summer was close, and the men had already been traveling for more than two months. "The march is growing terribly monotonous," Scott recorded in his journal.[179] Difficult though it was, they managed to pull at least eleven miles, aiming for double-digit travels, each day. "Our chance still holds good if we can put the work in," a hopeful Scott wrote on January 11, "but it is a terribly trying time."[180]

Bowers "continued in his indefatigable efforts" to determine their location with his sextant, though blizzards and clouds often veiled the sun.[181] By January 12, he had determined that they were less than sixty-three miles to the pole. On January 14, they camped a mere forty miles away.

The next night, January 15, they left a small depot with nine days of food and fuel. They were confident now that they would see the pole with only two more days of hauling ahead of them. Rather than excitement, however, exhaustion and a dread of the "appalling possibility of the sight of the Norwegian flag" colored their view. Still, Scott wrote, "we ought to do it now."[182]

On January 16, 1912, they were halfway through their afternoon march when Bowers saw a speck on the horizon.

No, no, the others argued! It was just a bit of sastrugi at a weird angle to the sun. Bowers let himself be convinced. He didn't really want to believe his eyes.

But they couldn't be blind for long. The black spot grew larger and larger.

A flag and dark tent were "near by the remains of a camp; sledge tracks and ski tracks going and coming and the clear trace of dogs' paws—many dogs," Scott recorded in his journal.[183] The British team had finally come upon the tracks they had been looking for. The Norwegians had found their own way to the pole.

The five men from Scott's team at the South Pole. Top row (left to right): Oates, Scott, Edgar Evans. Bottom Row: Bowers and Dr. Wilson.
[Henry Bowers/Wikimedia Commons]

The men were devastated, and Scott's diary is laced with grief:

> *"Great God! this is an awful place and terrible enough for us to have labored to it without the reward of priority."* [184]

All that could be done was to take navigational readings, lay their own marks, and hurry away. They had been beaten, and the only thing now was to leave.

They had made it to the pole, but their journey was only half over. Exhausted, injured, hungry, and cold—they now had to retrace the entire distance they had just traveled, and they had to do it alone. They were just five men, at the end of the earth, in a place where no other animal thought it fit to live. All they had was one another. They turned north on January 19, 1912.

There was one, final piece of inspiration that kept them going. Scott had hinted at it, barely putting the hope into words, the very day they had arrived at the pole and realized their defeat. He wrote in his journal, ending the entry for the horrible day: "Now for the run home and a desperate struggle to get the news through first. I wonder if we can do it."[185]

While Scott journeyed to the pole, the *Terra Nova* was on its way back to Cape Evans to resupply the camp. Maybe—just maybe!—if they were fast enough, Scott and his men could arrive back before she left. Perhaps they could be the ones to let the world know that *two* teams had reached the pole. The Norwegians had been first, but Scott's men had made it, and they had made it by the honest sweat of man-hauling. The man with the news would be the man who spun achievement.

Being the first to tell the world was not the only reason to hurry away. The men were developing altitude sickness: fierce headaches, nosebleeds, constant shortness of breath, dehydration. And, an inability to recover from injury.

Oates's big toe was black by the end of their third day heading

Dr. Wilson.
[Herbert Ponting/Library of Congress]

north, though he still told no one about it. Soon, his cheeks and nose were a sickly yellow, too. He was getting worse, and Scott once again noted that "Oates gets cold feet," where the rest of them were not so disturbed.[186] Edgar Evans's hand, too, kept filling with pus. Dr. Wilson treated it every other day, but it was obvious he was getting worse, too. In Scott's own reckoning, they had "a long way to go, and by Jove, this is tremendous labour."[187]

Edgar Evans's hand was a problem; but more than the injury, a change in attitude worried Scott. Edgar Evans had always been optimistic, like the rest of them. None of the men who were chosen for the pole were ones to shirk duty or sandbag the team with complaining.

But something had changed in Edgar Evans. He had begun to lose heart. "He is very much annoyed with himself," Scott wrote, "which is not a good sign."[188] For the first time, little discomforts, like losing fingernails, were not shrugged off. Whatever was ailing Edgar Evans's body had reached his mind. Scott could only hope that things would improve as they descended the glacier.

"I woke up to the sound of winds ricocheting off my tent so hard it sounded like there was a freight train rolling beside me. . . . It's a day when the most prudent thing may have been to roll over, go back to sleep and wait for tomorrow. However . . . there is a razor thin margin for error when it comes to carrying enough food. That means everyday [sic] I'm out here not moving yet still eating, I'm one day closer to running out of food and time."

~Colin O'Brady, November 29, 2018[189]

"Again another really challenging day—just when you think things can't get any harder, Antarctica decides to ramp it up to another level. So I came out of the tent this morning to complete whiteout conditions. So just zero visibility and I couldn't see the ground, whether I was standing on any undulations or anything. . . . Basically I was going to be in for a day of tackling essentially an icy obstacle course, blindfolded."

~Lou Rudd, November 14, 2018[190]

CHAPTER 10

THE POLE,

O'BRADY/RUDD: NOVEMBER 19, 2018– DECEMBER 14, 2018

Approaching Thiels Corner, Antarctica— Day 17—November 19, 2018

Colin's first thought upon waking was his mantra: "You are strong. You are capable."[191] Every morning, before he did anything else, he said it out loud. He often spoke about love, about inspiration, and he truly believed in both of those things. But the thought that got him going and kept him going was to win.

It was working. He was ahead.

Three days after he had reached the first waypoint, he reached the second. On Day 17, he saw the lonely outpost of Thiels Corner, a refueling depot maintained by ALE for their flights to and from the South Pole. It was barely anything, just a few fuel drums, a runway-clearing vehicle, and a small building without any people, but it was the first sign of humanity he had seen since passing Lou on Day 6.

Generally, silence didn't bother him. For years, he had participated in an annual ten-day Vipassana Meditation silent retreat. In Antarctica, he embraced the challenge of silence rather than running from it. It was a choice, though, not a mandate, and he celebrated reaching Thiels Corner by listening to Paul Simon's *Graceland* album all day: the full album on repeat six times through. Even while "loose and deep snow made for another day of slogging and slow going," the music lifted his spirits and kept him "dancing and smiling" as he hauled.[192]

He would use whatever tools suited him best—witnessing silence, celebrating milestones—to keep going. Farther. Faster.

S

Approaching Thiels Corner, Antarctica— Day 17—November 19, 2018

Lou knew Colin was ahead. It had been overconfidence, a bit of hubris, earlier. When he woke up and saw Colin skiing past that day, he had been stunned that the younger, less experienced explorer had managed that speed. "I had it in my head," he later said, "that I had pulled this massive lead on him."[193] To be honest, he was shocked that Colin was keeping it up.

Still, it was a long journey. Over the course of nine hundred miles,

Lou's little nineteen-mile deficit seemed almost inconsequential. If only he could keep it from growing.

He reached Thiels Corner on Day 18, a single day after Colin. The day was a complete whiteout, "thick and gloomy," he reported, and he was less than a mile away when the shapes of the depot seemed to materialize in front of him.[194] He had already skied a full day, but he pushed himself to keep going. He camped a mile past the marker, making and passing his goal.

For the most part, Lou was happy with his progress. He had upped his daily skiing time to eleven hours, and his mileage had increased with the time. Usually, he hauled for fifteen to seventeen miles, and he was thrilled to be pulling that much in the conditions he faced.

Getting going, though, was difficult. Mornings had always been his hardest time, even from his first expedition with Henry. On that trip, the thought of the coming pain and cold had made it impossible for him to eat breakfast, and he had dry-retched into the snow every day. It wasn't quite so bad anymore (he had stopped gagging at the thought of food), but mornings were invariably rough.

Lou followed the same routine, every day. He lit his cooking stove before he got out of his sleeping bag and began melting snow for water. Then, he ran outside in just his thermal leggings to relieve himself —even in Antarctica, nature calls!—digging a hole six inches below the surface and cleaning himself with chunks of ice. It was ". . . super-grim. Probably the worst task of the daily routine," Lou confessed.[195] Coming back inside, he ate his porridge breakfast, dismantled his tent, and packed everything into the pulk. Finally, he hooked his harness to the load and began his eleven hours of hauling. He had the routine down to an art, and the entire process took him less than an hour and a half.

Day 20 began like every other. He woke up. He lit the stove. He pooped. He ate and packed. But on Day 20, when Lou hooked his harness to the pulk and pulled, his pulk pulled back.

It didn't move.

It had "pretty much snowed all through the night, and it was still snowing this morning" when he woke up, Lou said, and inches of fresh powder were like wet cement, anchoring the pulk to the ground.[196] He jerked and tugged. With all of his strength, he managed to move mere inches. It took him a full thirty minutes to travel a scant quarter mile. Something had to change.

He had never portaged before, but he had heard other explorers talk about it. The idea was to make his sled lighter by leaving half his gear where he was, skiing on a bit with a lightened load, dropping that load, turning around, and then returning for the rest. It meant skiing three miles for every one mile of true progress, but it was the only way he could make headway in such deep snow.

He unpacked the pulk and removed forty days of food. Then, he tagged the spot in his GPS, using the precise coordinates to make sure that he could always find his way back. Just for good measure, he stuck a ski upright in the snow, too.

This time, when he pulled, the pulk moved. "It was easy to zip along with half the load," Lou remembered. "Visibility was all right at that point. You could see a mile on the horizon, and the pulk felt fantastic."[197] He flew down the plain. After he had gone about a mile, he took out the rest of his gear and turned around to get his food. His deep tracks were easy to follow in the snow on a clear afternoon. Soon, he was back at his original drop. He loaded up the food and easily skied forward to where he had left the rest.

It had worked so well that Lou immediately did it again. He kept his pulk packed with the food, stuck a ski upright in the snow once again, and skied on.

But, he had made a desperate mistake. He had forgotten to tag the drop on his GPS.

By the time Lou skied one mile from the drop point, the wind had picked up. All of the loose snow on the ground was blown in a dizzying madness of white and wind. Visibility, which had been a full mile for the last trip, was down to thirty feet.

He turned around. Nothing. "I can't believe I can't see my tracks," he thought, fighting panic as he realized he had forgotten the GPS tag.[198]

Lou fell to his knees, searching the ground, pressing his face into the blizzard, hunting for any hint of his path. Everything had been wiped away.

He had no tent. He had no sleeping bag. Alone, facing a blizzard, Lou would freeze. Instantly, it became "a survival situation," he said.[199]

He was a seasoned explorer; he had faced perilous situations before. But all he could think was: "This is getting quite dangerous . . . Nobody is coming to get me in these conditions."[200] The ALE plane couldn't land in a storm, and the weather could last for days. Without his tent or his sleeping bag, he would die.

He had to find his gear.

Using his compass and dead reckoning, Lou began to ski back north. In the swirling, blinding snow, Lou kept searching, barely skiing forward as he stared into the abyss in every direction.

His one hope was the lone ski standing straight. The snow would've already covered his bags. If the ski was no longer standing straight, the day would be fatal.

Ever so slowly, he continued forward. The mile seemed endless.

By pure luck, Lou turned. At just the right moment, just as a gap opened in the spindrift, he looked over his shoulder. There, a few hundred feet away, almost behind him, his lone ski still stood tall, marking the ground.

Relief coursed through him.

He never should have kept his tent and his sleeping bag together; he should have traveled with one while leaving the other at a drop. It was an oversight that came from attempting a technique he had never done before and hadn't thought through. And he had nearly died because of it.

Lou gathered his gear, made his way back to the food, and collapsed into his tent. He was only two miles from his campsite the night before. But he would live to tell the story.

S

On the polar plateau, Antarctica— Day 27—November 29, 2018

Colin was twenty-seven miles ahead of Lou—almost two days of travel.

The winds were brutal, and he had entered yet another field of sastrugi. Yet he was still moving. In spite of it all, Colin kept pulling and kept going forward.

That is, right until the moment the skins covering the bottom of his skis ripped off and his skis slid out from underneath him. The skins acted like a ratchet, smoothly sliding in one direction, but baring teeth and acting as a brake when pushed in the other direction.

Without skins, he had no traction. He had no grip to haul the pulk. Colin was "stopped dead in [his] tracks."[201]

He had a spare set of skins, but attaching them to his skis meant that he needed to set up the tent. In the howling wind, he needed the tent's protection to find the spare, glue it on, and wait for the glue to dry. It was a simple repair, but it meant hours and hours of preparation and setup. And he hadn't thought to bring a spare pair of skis, like Lou.

Four miles into his day, Colin was done. By the time he got everything set up and repaired, and the glue dried, it was so late in the day as to be pointless to dismantle his camp and ski on.

The delay had caused him to lose twelve miles off his lead. It was, he recalled, "the most challenging and frustrating day" yet.[202] Less than a day's travel now separated the two men.

Just north of the polar plateau, Antarctica—Day 30—December 2, 2018

The days that followed his portage attempt were rough, but the winds had hardened the snow somewhat, and Lou was at least able to move his fully laden pulk.

On Day 30, Lou fought deep sastrugi in the morning as he climbed his final feet to the polar plateau. Then, in the afternoon, he pushed through hours of complete whiteout conditions. The month of constant motion through long days of blindness had left him physically, mentally, and emotionally spent.

Then, just as exhaustion threatened to drown his ambition, he noticed something out of the corner of his eye. A small bird, "pure white . . . about the size of a dove, with a little black beak, literally fluttering right in front of me," Lou recalled. It fought the wind, and "it was equally as intrigued by me as I was by it."[203] It should have been impossible for anything to be alive so far from the coast. Yet here they were—bird and man—they had found each other.

Then the wind picked up, and the bird was caught in the breeze.

"I'm not a particularly spiritual person," Lou wrote, "but if ever there was anyone coming to pay me a visit and have a look, that was it. . . . If it was someone, I know exactly who It [sic] was."[204]

It was just what Lou needed to keep going. Day after day, Lou

Snow petrel flying in Antarctica. [Ilya Grigorik/Wikimedia Commons]

kept pushing through in sixteen- and seventeen-mile days. On Day 33, he crossed 88°S and finally reached the polar plateau. Now, with the major climbing behind him, he could really put on some speed.

He would have to, if he was going to catch Colin.

S

Polar plateau, Antarctica— Day 32—December 4, 2018

Colin had reached the polar plateau on Day 32. In the days since his skins had ripped off the skis, he had regained a more than twenty-mile lead over Lou. Every day, he skied two or three miles farther than Lou. The difference wasn't much, but it added up.

They used the term "skiing," because that's what they wore: skis. Yet the slow plodding across the ice and through the snow was hardly like downhill skiing or even the efficient glide of cross-country skis. "It's like two tortoises racing each other," Colin later quipped.[205]

It was more like snowshoeing than anything. The skis simply helped spread out the skier's weight across the surface and pro-tected them against weak spots in the ice. Extra grip from the skins helped them across slick surfaces, but their pace was anything but fast.

Up on the polar plateau, the air was thinner, and the weather was colder, but at least he wasn't pulling uphill so much. The flat terrain was a welcome relief. Colin was grateful, always grateful. And he was buoyed by the love that was sent by followers from around the world.

Through his yearly silent Vipassana retreats, he had become convinced that "we possess the power to project and feel beyond our basic five senses." Enveloped in silence, Colin believed that he could "feel the energy of others very strongly."[206] Thousands of miles away from his family, Colin perceived their support, and he tried to send it back out to the world as well.

Sometimes, however, the motivation and inspiration to keep going was right in front of him. On clear days when the sun and the sky were just right, a rainbow encircled the sun. Called a parhelion, it brought Colin to a standstill, "committing all of the senses of that moment to memory."[207] Sometimes, Antarctica's beauty was greater than its suffering.

Parhelion (also called a sun halo or sun dog). [Scott Woolums/ALE]

On other days, Colin's inspiration was a direct result of one human being caring for another.

December 6, 2018, had been a long day for Colin. He had hauled for twelve hours and had plodded through another seventeen miles. At the end of it, all he wanted to do was to talk to Jenna and go to sleep.

They had their call, just like they did every night. But, at the end of their conversation, Jenna told him he wasn't done—she gave him a phone number and told him to call it. That night. Right then.

He protested—he was tired, he needed sleep—but Jenna insisted. Just call. Trust her. Somewhat begrudgingly, Colin agreed.

"Hello," he said, when the call went through. "This is Colin, from Antarctica."

"Hi, this is Paul," the other voice said.

Colin paused, confused as to whether he should recognize the voice and the name.

The voice on the other end continued, "Yeah, Paul Simon."

Colin thought he was hallucinating. "Am I really sitting in the middle of Antarctica, on my satellite phone, talking to Paul Simon—have I completely lost my mind!"

It was true. Paul Simon—fifteen-time Grammy winner, half of the duo Simon & Garfunkel, and recipient of Kennedy Center Honors—was on the phone. "Shocked" and "stunned" didn't seem to do it justice.[208]

Their conversation wended its way through creativity and the process of giving every ounce of yourself to art. Paul's art was clearly music, but more and more Colin had begun to think of himself as an artist as well. Later, he would explain that he thought of his "canvas [as] endurance sport."[209] They were different forms of art—music and sports—but both Paul Simon and Colin knew what it meant to perform at the elite, highest levels. The conversation lifted his spirits higher than the plateau.

The next day, Colin danced through his hours of hauling.

And the day after that, he crossed 89°S, the last degree before the pole.

He had done this part of the journey before, during the Explorers Grand Slam. It had felt hard then, and he hadn't already pulled a pulk for thirty-six days. But he wasn't the same person now as he had been in 2016.

Just three days after crossing the final degree, he camped mere miles away from the pole.

On Day 40, Colin skied the last three miles and reached the Amundsen-Scott South Pole Station and ceremonial marker for the South Pole at 10:00 a.m. Chilean time. He later remembered that "it was this beautiful sunny day, actually, this kind of calm day where I had these tears of joy rolling down my face."[210] That night, he posted on Instagram: "I expected to be happy reaching the South Pole, but today has quite honestly been one of the best days of my entire life."[211]

The weather made it seem like the whole world was celebrating with him. Even from thousands of miles away, he once again felt "all of the love that was being sent my way from all over the world. Deep, deep, deep gratitude—I'm shining my love right back at you."[212]

The research station was fully staffed in the Antarctic summer, and a few scientists came out to take his picture and cheer him on. More would have come out, but, for them, it was the middle of the night.

Time zones converge at the South Pole, and people follow the time of the country from which they departed. Colin, having left from Punta Arenas, was on Chilean time. The US scientists who worked at

Ceremonial South Pole (permanent marker) with the Amundsen-Scott South Pole Station in the background. [Bill Spindler/Wikimedia Commons]

the research base had all traveled from Christchurch, New Zealand. It was 10:00 a.m. for Colin, but, for the scientists in the very same place, it was 2:00 a.m. the next morning.

Colin didn't stay long at the pole. It was too tempting to be around even this sliver of civilization. So he moved on.

He hooked back into his harness and pulled again for the horizon, finally headed north once again.

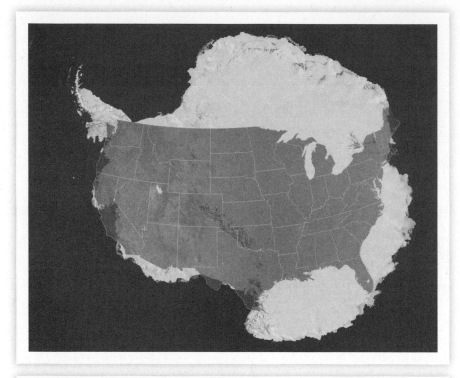

The continental forty-eight United States overlaid on a satellite image of Antarctica. [NASA]

S

Approaching the South Pole, Antarctica— Day 38—December 10, 2018

Every day was a fight.

But Lou kept going.

Every night, he would look down at his GPS and be slightly amazed at the distance he had covered. It felt like he hadn't gone anywhere, yet every day, he found that he had moved. He hadn't had a full rest day since he began, more than a month ago. But Lou kept pulling on.

Antarctica was just so big. If it were laid on top of the United States, it would more than cover the continental forty-eight states. On Day 38, Lou crossed paths with an ALE caravan traveling overland from the South Pole back to Union Glacier. A huge, custom truck outfitted with crawler treads pulled three sleds of gear. Even with all that power, it would still take the caravan six days to reach Union Glacier.

But for Lou, the South Pole was mere days away. Whiteouts dropped deep snow, and the thin atmosphere made him work for every breath. Yet on Day 40, Lou camped just eleven miles away. It was "really exciting—sort of like Christmas," he said.[213] Whatever weather the next day brought, he was going to push to make it.

He woke up at 4:00 a.m. In another whiteout day, he couldn't see

Geographic South Pole. Because ice is not stationary, the researchers at the South Pole take new measurements and locate the absolute pole every January 1. [John Beatty/ALE]

anything on the horizon. But at 4:45 p.m., Chilean time, he arrived at the bottom of the world.

"Absolutely epic day!" Lou's voice was taut with excitement when he called home. Researchers poured out from the station, and the station manager herself came out with hugs and cheers. They had all been following his journey, and their excitement at his arrival—all the pictures, the hugs, the congratulations, and the encouragement— made him "feel like quite a celebrity," he said.[214]

When he spoke with the ALE guide stationed at the pole, he heard once again about all the people who had been forced to give up their own expeditions in light of the horrible weather and deep snow. Colin was still ahead of him, but Lou's stubborn determination to keep going was getting him the miles where almost no one else could.

Before he left the pole, he went through his gear and took stock of what he had left, making sure he had enough to go on. His clothes had started to feel loose long ago. But he had expected that. It was unpleasant, but Lou was mostly healthy. He had planned correctly, and no shortage of food would make another Englishman turn back.

For Lou, it was only onward and northward to the finish.

S

North of the South Pole, en route to Leverett Glacier, Antarctica— Day 42—December 14, 2018

Colin was ravenous. "I'm looking down at my body," he told Jenna during their nightly call, "and I don't recognize it . . . my wrist watch is sliding around on my arm."[215]

He had known it was coming. He had planned and built up his weight, knowing he was going to lose so much that his body would become a stranger.

But it's easier to know that, to plan for it, than to feel it. It is always tempting to preempt the reality of here and now to a future pain.

Back at Union Glacier, Colin had been faced with the reality of the pulk. He had barely been able to move it during his initial practice runs at base camp. To make his pulling more manageable, he had decided some weight would have to come off. As a last-minute decision, he had left three and a half days of food at base camp.

At the pole, he had looked over his supplies, just as Lou had. He had counted and compared what he had left with the journey ahead; he had realized how tight of a race it would be.

It wasn't Lou that Colin was now worried about. It was starvation.

"*Before we began our march all unnecessary clothes were taken off and put on the sledges. It almost looked as if everything would be considered superfluous, and the costume in which we finally started would no doubt have been regarded as somewhat unseemly in our latitudes. We smiled and congratulated ourselves that at present no ladies had reached the Antarctic regions, or they might have objected to our extremely comfortable and serviceable costume.*"

~*Roald Amundsen, January 3, 1912* [216]

"*I wonder what is in store for us, with some little alarm at the lateness of the season.*"

~ *Captain Scott, March 8, 1912* [217]

CHAPTER 11

THE RETURN,
AMUNDSEN/SCOTT:
JANUARY 1912–MARCH 1912

Polar plateau, Antarctica—January 1, 1912

Headed north and away from the pole, Amundsen and his men braced for the Devil's Ballroom. The memories of the black-depth crevasses, the giant hummocks of ice, and the long, tortuous route that bled time and energy were fresh in their minds. One way or another, they would have to make it through again.

Until, suddenly, they realized they were past it. They had worried and fretted until one night they looked through their binoculars and saw the worst areas already behind them, to the south. "With incredible luck we had slipped past all those ugly and dangerous places," Amundsen later said.[218] They had unknowingly veered from their previous course, and, somehow, they had managed to avoid the dreaded landscape.

Clearly, they were not following their previous course. They were traveling fast, using a sail to harness the wind and propel them forward as they killed dogs for food. Between the dog meat and pemmican, food wasn't an issue—they had plenty of it. Their journey was so successful and so smooth that finding the depots came down to pride. They all wanted to have the bragging rights of saying they found every depot they had laid.

So when they saw they had skied past the last depot on the plateau, they "stood there expressing our annoyance rather forcibly," Amundsen said.[219] Every one of Amundsen's men volunteered to ski the fifteen miles back to it.

Amundsen chose Hanssen and Bjaaland for the trip. With an empty sled and a full team, they covered the distance in only ten hours. The extra thirty miles, plus what they had already done during their regular journey, put them at more than fifty miles traveled in one day. It was an amazing feat for both men and dogs.

Traveling home was entirely different from the journey to the pole. Heading north, "the weather was radiantly clear," Amundsen wrote. On the way to the pole, the men had slept lightly to wake as soon as there was a fleeting moment of sunshine; on the way home, they had "the brightest, clearest weather," Amundsen remembered.[220] Which, unfortunately, made everything look wholly unfamiliar.

New mountains kept popping up. Entire peaks they had completely missed on their way to the pole now crowded the horizon. Even the ones they had managed to see and name looked so different in the sunlight that the men were stunned when they realized a "new" mountain was really an old landmark. Amundsen declared, "I would

One of the dog teams and sledges from Amundsen's expedition. The dog driver either skied alongside or rode on top of the load. [Library of Congress]

readily have taken my most solemn oath that I had never seen that landscape before in my life."[221]

Truthfully, he hadn't seen it. The irony was that good weather, not bad, was preventing the men from finding their bearings. It was almost—*almost*—like they were lost.

Because once again, four days after Hanssen's and Bjaaland's ultramarathon, they couldn't find a depot. This, however, was not just any minor landmark stop. This time, they couldn't find the Butcher's Shop.

It was their biggest drop; they had loaded it with dog meat and gear. Yet, "it was not so much for the sake of the food it contained that we considered it so necessary to find this spot, as [it was] for discovering the way down to the Barrier again," Amundsen explained.[222] The Butcher's Shop marked their trail to descend the mountain. They had to find it.

On January 4, they *should* have come across it. They had traveled the miles. They had followed the right course, or so they thought. So, where was it? Again, each man pulled out binoculars.

At the edge of the plateau, looking down through the mountains, they could just see the Barrier ice, far off in the distance. But, the mountains that separated them from the land below looked entirely unfamiliar. It was the same story that had plagued them for days. It was as though magic—witchcraft, even!—had placed them in a new world, and they could not figure out how to get down to the Barrier below. They looked and looked in a continuous sea of white.

Until Hanssen cried out, "Hullo!"

"Yes!" Wisting joined in, seeing the same thing. "I'm hanged if that isn't my broken ski that I stuck up by the depot."[223]

Right next to a small mound, which looked like any other mound among thousands of others that rose and fell at the top of sheer cliffs, a black mark stuck out of the snow. Wisting's afterthought, a last-minute gesture as they left camp, had saved them. Mercifully, the lone ski managed to stand out amid a field of white.

It was easy enough to get there, now that they knew where they were headed. When they arrived, the meat was still frozen and their gear was still in place. The men were not extraordinarily hungry, but the ravenous dogs looked "rather surprised," Amundsen said, at how much food was offered to them.[224] Just as with their last time at the Butcher's Shop, the dogs ate until they could not eat anymore.

Unlike last time, however, they did not stop here to rest. As soon as the dogs were fed, the men repacked the sledges, and then they moved on. No one wanted to stay a moment longer than necessary; the Butcher's Shop would always be a sorrowful place for them, haunted by the sacrifice of their canine friends.

The way down the glacier only made the men more impressed with the strength of the dogs that had made the way up the same path. Several times on that first day alone, "the pace became so great that we had to stop and put brakes under the sledges," Amundsen wrote as they wrapped rope around the sledge runners once again.[225]

Olav Bjaaland in his expedition outfit. [National Library of Norway]

By the time they ended their day's march, they had descended nearly 2,000 feet, and already Amundsen thought, "I could notice a difference in my breathing; it seemed to work much more easily and pleasantly."[226] Clear weather continued to light their journey, and they saw that following the glacier, rather than zigzagging their way through the mountains as they had on the ascent, would take them directly down to the Barrier. They decided that they would gladly trade a longer route back to Framheim on the Barrier for a safer passage through the mountains.

Sure enough, the rest of Axel Heiburg Glacier was so smooth that the men on skis sped past the dog teams. They crossed onto the Great Barrier once again on January 6, 1912, having spent fifty-one days over land.

From here to 80°S, they had depots marking their course with food and fuel at every degree. At the first depot, they were surprised to find the food was rotten. The air was freezing, but the sun must have warmed the food to the point of spoiling. It was unfortunate, but it didn't really matter—they had plenty of food with them already.

The men were all healthy; the dogs were all pulling hard. Soon, they picked up their line of Barrier beacons, the snow cairns that marked the route from one depot to another. On the outbound, southern journey, Amundsen had placed notes in each with headings leading to the next, more northerly beacon. Now, homeward bound, they breathed a sigh of relief every time they saw one, glad of the confirmation they were on the right heading. They would often camp for the night next to these guides, friends, pointing the way home.

On January 9, their first sign of life from the coast flew into view as two skua gulls glided over the horizon, "to our unspeakable astonishment," Amundsen remembered. The pair circled overhead, landed on the beacon, and flew off to the south a few moments later. "They brought us a message from the living world into this realm of death—a message of all that was dear to us," Amundsen wrote.[227]

At 4:00 a.m. on January 25, 1912, the first man arrived at Framheim, waiting to enter the hut until every man skied into camp. They had left together, they had been victorious together, and they would return again, together.

When they did open the door, the others at Framheim looked at them as if they were ghosts. Finally, someone spoke:

"What about the Pole? Have you been there?"

"Yes, of course; otherwise you would hardly have seen us again."

Skua gull flying in Antarctica. [Eli Duke via Flickr [CC BY-SA2.0]]

Then, with handshakes and cheers all around, they made pancakes and coffee. As Amundsen said, "it was good outside, but still better at home."[228]

S

Top of the Beardmore Glacier, Antarctica—February 6, 1912

Luck was not with Scott. It seemed as though it hadn't been the entire trip, and nothing had changed since the pole.

The men were falling apart. Oates's leg was getting worse, though he hadn't told anyone about his pain. Dr. Wilson had pulled a tendon in his own leg, and, on top of it, he had snow blindness that stung so badly he couldn't sleep at night. Scott had hurt his shoulder in a spectacular fall and became "another sick person added to our tent," he wrote.[229]

Then there was Edgar Evans. His fingers were full of pus, his fingernails had fallen off, and his hands were spotted with blisters. And, just as they were approaching Beardmore Glacier, he took two bad falls into crevasses. He had hit his head—once? twice?—and he had been acting strangely ever since.

Bowers, strong, indestructible Bowers, was the only one who seemed fit.

Scott just wanted to be done with the plateau. They had been at altitude for "forty-eight days—nearly seven weeks in low temperature with almost incessant wind," he wrote. "Food is low and weather uncertain."[230] They were hungry, cold, injured, and miserable.

Little did they know that things were about to get worse.

These cliffs of rock flank Beardmore Glacier. Here, in 2016, people are "geologizing" as Scott did. [Allan C. Ashworth and Terry L. Erwin/Wikimedia Commons]

The next day, on February 7, at the top of Beardmore Glacier, they found their Upper Glacier Depot. But when they took stock of the food, a full day's worth of rations was just . . . gone.

Had Teddy Evans's party taken more than they were supposed to? Had the wrong amount been stored to begin with? It was no use laying blame; nothing could be done about it now. But if anything happened to slow their journey to the next depot, they would have to cut into their already paltry portions.

It was a "wretched day," Scott wrote.[231] They needed to move—fast—to the next depot and get more food.

Instead, incredibly, they spent part of each of the next two days "geologizing," Scott said. He just couldn't resist the pull of bare rock. "[I]t is like going ashore after a sea voyage," he wrote, just to be able to touch something that wasn't snow or ice. The discoveries were "obviously so interesting," that searching for fossils and retrieving specimens took precedence over their injuries, exhaustion, and lack of food.[232] It was the one time his writing was more than miserable stoicism.

They added thirty-five pounds of rocks to their sledges. (Amid the hundreds of pounds they were already carrying, the additional weight barely made a difference.) But science couldn't get them any closer to home. Even Scott's enthusiasm for discovery couldn't blind them for long. They had no choice but to continue pulling and start down the maze of danger on Beardmore Glacier.

They had only two more days' worth of food with them.

Their next depot was close—it *should* have been less than a two days' journey away—but "if this weather doesn't clear by tomorrow, we must either march blindly on or reduce food," Scott wrote on February 10.[233] Half rations were always a possibility, but the men were rapidly losing weight even while eating their full allotment each day.

February 11 was even worse. The small crevasses abruptly turned into "the worst ice mess I have ever been in . . . huge chasms, closely packed and most difficult to cross."[234] They wandered, lost, in the sea of peaks and gashes, first going east, then turning again west, trying to find a route down the mountains. The men fought over which way was best, their small bickering arguments showing their fatigue.

The depot was nowhere in sight. They had no choice; they had to conserve their food. The next day's midday meal would have to be both lunch and dinner.

The men, already weak, began to grow weaker. Even full rations were not enough, and they tore through the half rations. They needed to rest, but, as Scott wrote, "we cannot do the distance without the hours." By February 12, Scott realized that they were "in a very critical situation."[235]

They were only halfway down the glacier.

Gradually, the crevasse fields disappeared and the surface became easier to navigate. Daily, they descended and lost some of the altitude that had only magnified their weakness. But as the glacier lost its terror, Scott only began to fear even more for his men.

Edgar Evans had not improved. Even the lower altitude did not help. Nearly every day, Scott recorded his concerns: "Evans is the chief anxiety now . . . he shows considerable signs of being played out;"[236] "Evans . . . is going steadily downhill;"[237] "Evans . . . is giving us serious anxiety."[238]

Edgar Evans's spirits had never been high since he injured his hand, but they had withered more since his falls. He had become dull, unfocused, and incapable around the sled. Even when they stopped, Scott wrote, "Evans has no power to assist with camping work." He just sat and wouldn't—couldn't—help.[239] He was hungry. They were all hungry, but the injured man could not bear up.

Two days later, on February 14, after they had descended still farther, Edgar Evans stopped the rest of the men in the middle of hauling, first in the morning and again in the afternoon. He said that he needed something . . . or something else . . . The men couldn't understand his mumbling, confused speech. But what he said didn't really matter—they all knew what he wanted. He wanted to stop going on.

On February 17, Evans couldn't pull the sledge. They had nearly reached the bottom of the glacier, and all of the difficult terrain was behind them. But Edgar Evans couldn't haul. The others gave him skis and asked him simply to follow in their tracks. Hour by hour, he slipped farther behind.

At the end of the day, the others retraced their steps. They found Evans "on his knees with clothing disarranged, hands uncovered and frostbitten, and a wild look in his eyes. . . . He showed every sign of complete collapse," Scott wrote.[240]

They laid him on the empty sledge and began to haul him back to camp. By the time they reached the tent, Edgar Evans was dead.

There was no burial. Digging was hard work; for the starving men, any extra movement that did not lead forward was wasted. But there was relief for Scott and the three remaining. Scott wrote, "it is a terrible thing to lose a companion in this way, but calm reflection shows that there could not have been a better ending to the terrible anxieties of the past week. . . . what a desperate pass we were in with a sick man on our hands so far from home."[241]

They had lost a friend, yes, but they had also lost a human's worth of responsibility. They had not been able to abandon Edgar Evans while there was any hope still left, even as he slowed them down and made tragedy more likely for them all. Now, that weight was lifted.

They pushed on. They had no other choice.

The next day, they found Shambles Camp and the pony meat; it was the mark of the Great Barrier. They were done with the pole, done with the plateau, done with the glacier. They were down from the high altitude and back on level ice.

With a smaller, lighter sledge, and the promise of frequent depots along the way, all they had to do was average 8.6 miles a day on a flat surface in order to reach the huge stores of supplies at One Ton Depot before they ran out of food and fuel. With the pony meat from Shambles Camp, they were back to full rations and would be able to "continue a more plentiful era if we can keep good marches up," Scott wrote.[242]

The ground conditions were awful, and for the first few days they only managed to haul for a few miles. But even with these meager distances, they found their first Barrier depot on February 22. Their spirits soared when first seeing the depot cairn, yet they fell twice as hard when the men took stock

Lawrence "Titus" Oates.
[Herbert Ponting/Wikimedia Commons]

of the supplies. The meat had rotted. The fuel canisters were almost empty.

Somehow, the fuel had evaporated or leaked. "Things must be critical till we reach the [next] depot," Scott wrote in his journal.[243] The weak, cold men would now only have heat for cooking and never just for warmth.

And then the temperature dropped. First the low was -20°F. Then -30°F. Then -40°F. And it stayed cold. Without fuel for heat, the temperature inside their tent at night was only one or two degrees warmer than outside.

At the next depot, on March 1, the fuel cans were barely more than fumes. Again. Even with the "most rigid economy," Scott wrote, "it can scarce carry us to the next depot."[244]

Scott had always paired his misery with some amount of redemption. But now, there was no way to soften the fatality of their situation. He had not planned an emergency fund of either food or fuel. They stretched the food, and they would stretch it more if needed. But fuel was warmth and life. They couldn't simply water it down.

To one another, they kept up lighthearted appearances. They joked. They told stories. But, in his heart, Scott knew that a desperate situation had gotten even worse. The surface was "covered with sandy frostrime," he wrote, and they had to pull against it with all their strength to move the sledge.[245] He confessed to his journal, "God help us. We can't keep up this pulling, that is certain. Amongst ourselves we are unendingly cheerful, but what each man feels in his heart I can only guess."[246]

The missing supplies were enough to seal their fate, but Scott wrote truthfully on March 2 that "misfortunes rarely come singly."

Oates could no longer keep his pain to himself. They called Oates "The Soldier," and, true to his name, Oates had walked on, concealing his injuries until his feet had become "very bad indeed."[247]

Every morning, it took him an hour and a half to stuff his agonizingly tender, frostbitten feet into his boots. And then, every step was misery. Still, The Soldier was stoic, and Scott wrote that Oates "is wonderfully plucky, as his feet must be giving him great pain. He makes no complaint, but his spirits only come in spurts now, and he grows more silent in the tent."[248]

By March 7, Scott wrote, "One feels that for poor Oates the crisis is near."[249] Oates himself asked Dr. Wilson three days later if there was any chance of him living through the journey, but the doctor could only reply that nothing was for certain.

Though Oates was the worst off, Scott wrote on March 10 with blunt honesty, "I doubt whether we could get through." There was always a chance, however slim, but the reality was that "the weather conditions are awful, and our gear gets steadily more icy and difficult to manage." They had found another depot, but it was "cold comfort. Shortage on our allowance all round."[250] The food was rotten and the fuel was gone. Again.

They were fifty-five miles from the salvation of supplies at One Ton Depot with only seven days of food left. They knew not to expect a miracle.

On March 11, they divided the supply of opium tablets in their medical kit. Dr. Wilson, Bowers, and Oates each got thirty pills and Scott took a vial of morphine. Death from starvation and freezing was neither easy nor fast. If he wanted it, each man now had a way of avoiding that death with another, quicker one. Suicide would mean that they had given up all hope. But it also would free them from pain. They would each have to decide how they wanted to perish.

"Titus Oates," Scott wrote, "is very near the end."[251]

The skies darkened, and every day they had trouble seeing the way forward. Warmth never came. Oates's hands as well as his feet became useless. He was dependent on the others for everything from feeding to getting dressed.

They never managed to haul more than seven miles a day.

On March 16, Oates went to sleep, hoping not to wake in the morning. When he did, he asked the others to write to his mother for him. Then, leaving behind his boots for his friends, he opened the tent flap and walked out into the white. He called behind him, "I'm just going outside and may be some time."[252]

They never found his body.

The blizzards came. Scott's right foot froze, and only three days after Oates walked to his death, Scott became bound to the tent. They were eleven miles south of One Ton Depot.

Bowers was the strongest, and he and Dr. Wilson first made plans to run for the supplies together, coming back for Scott. And then, when Dr. Wilson's leg failed him, Bowers thought to go ahead alone.

Scott brought a professional photographer, Herbert Ponting, who captured dramatic portraits of the men. Ponting took this picture of Scott on his return from the stressful depot-laying trip of 1911.
[Herbert Ponting/Wikimedia Commons]

Blizzards, day after day, ruined each plan.

On March 20, they made their last cups of tea. On March 29, Scott wrote in his journal for the final time.

> *"It seems a pity, but I do not think I can write more—*
>
> *R. Scott*
>
> *Last entry. For God's sake look after our people."*[253]

Captain Robert Falcon Scott then lay down between Dr. Edward Adrian Wilson and Henry Robertson Bowers.

The three friends died, together.

"But the hairy truth of it is . . . I've lost a ton of weight. So much so that I am afraid to take a close look at my body. My calves feel more like the size of my arms at this point."

~Colin O'Brady, December 16, 2018[254]

"And my God, I've lost some weight. I've got abs for the first time in a very long time. My legs are like chicken legs. I reckon I've lost over 10kgs [about 22 lbs.] already."

~Lou Rudd, December 15, 2018[255]

CHAPTER 12

THE RETURN,

O'BRADY/RUDD: DECEMBER 13, 2018– DECEMBER 28, 2018

Eighteen miles north of the South Pole—
Day 41—December 13, 2018

Colin was desperate. He had left extra—what he thought was extra—food behind at Union Glacier.

Now, with that decision six hundred miles behind him and with another three hundred miles left to go, he didn't know if his food would last. Ben Saunders had quit at the pole, and Colin had just narrowly avoided doing the same. Back at the South Pole camp, Colin had counted his food and reviewed the numbers with the ALE guide stationed there. They had decided he could go on, he didn't need to quit—yet. But the finish was anything but certain.

"Every calorie is precious," he wrote on Instagram.[256] And he called for help.

Over his satellite phone, he gave Jenna and his mom an inventory of what food he had. It wasn't much.

Back in Oregon, Jenna and his mom spent the entire weekend crunching numbers. How much did they need to decrease his calories? How much could they cut while still giving him the energy to pull the weight of the pulk? What could he change to make the food last, while still giving him enough strength to go on?

They reported back: Already gut-wrenchingly hungry, Colin had to lower his daily intake by 900 calories, from 7,000 to 6,100 calories per day. And he had to ski. Fast.

On the reduced-calorie diet, Colin's mental battles would only become harder. Loss of food affected the brain as much as the rest of the body. Still, Colin increased his hauling time, upping it to thirteen hours each day. With the longer days, his mileage rose; he was now regularly covering twenty or more miles a day. He was still climbing very gradually, until, on Day 45, he hit the highest elevation of the whole journey at 9,649 feet.

The elevation leveled off, but life did not get any easier. On Day 47, he entered the region nicknamed Sastrugi National Park. And he reached it during a whiteout. With fifty-mile-per-hour winds.

The land between 88°S and 87°S was infamous for the dramatic waves of ice ridges. Instead of the two- or three-foot height he had faced on the climb to the South Pole, here the sastrugi rose to four and even sometimes six feet high. The climb up each ridge was challenging, and the drop on the far side was fear itself. Had it been good weather, Colin might have been able to see the edge and brace himself, but in the whiteout, the ground simply fell away.

That morning, hunger, exhaustion, pain, and fear nearly bound him to his tent. It was hard to see what could be gained from fighting against the sastrugi in blinding conditions while trying to haul several hundred pounds. He wrote on Instagram that "the voice in my head told me to stop, wait out the storm, rest. But the other voice told me I needed to keep moving forward or I'll run out of food. My mind was ripping me apart."[257]

He closed his eyes and spent a few minutes meditating. Though it couldn't change the weather, it "calmed the storm in my mind." He went out, "with renewed resolve," knowing that he was going to "battle hard with my personal demons."[258]

He managed to ski twenty-one and a half miles.

The next day, he went and did it again.

The winds had gotten worse through the night, "blowing consistently 35 mph, with gusts over 55 mph,"[259] he reported on Instagram. Over and over, Colin fell, first pummeled by the wind and then dropped by crests of sastrugi that disappeared without warning. It was frustrating, and it was dangerous.

Somehow, in all of his falls, he hadn't broken any equipment. Somehow, he hadn't gotten injured.

It was only a matter of time until his luck ran out.

As Colin fought his way across a particularly steep ridge, he felt his skis slide away with a smooth, unnatural glide. In a moment of terror, his feet slipped from underneath him, and he careened down the other side of the ice wave, falling into the pit between crests. Then Colin looked up and realized that his pulk was not next to him.

Far above, the heavy sled teetered on the edge of a massive ridge, directly above his leg. His skis pinned him to the ground.

Colin couldn't move as the pulk kept slowly rising and falling above him.

Somehow, the pulk didn't come crashing down. Miraculously, it stayed put. If it had fallen, it would have been "broken leg, broken ski, in a sastrugi storm," he recalled.[260] He was alone, with no hope of rescue for days.

Physically, he was fine. His skis, though, were not. The skins had torn away. They were "impossibly hard to reattach in the storm," Colin later said.[261] He had only been skiing for an hour, but he had no choice other than to set up his tent, start his stove, warm the air, reattach the skins, and wait for the glue to dry.

The last time this had happened, Colin spent the rest of the afternoon in his tent, relaxing and letting some of the fatigue ease out of his body. But now he barely had enough food to make it to the finish, even if he skied every day. He couldn't just waste the day in his tent.

"This too shall pass"—it was one of his favorite mantras, and Colin repeated it to himself again and again.[262] It took him almost an hour and a half once the glue was dry to repack his tent in the furious wind. It had already been an arduous, terrifying, slow, and boring day by turns. And he was barely past his campsite from the night before. It was the lowest moment of the journey.

But surely things would change.

And they did.

Moments after repeating his mantra, Colin got a text from a friend, quoting his favorite book, *The Alchemist*:

> On your quest to become one with your personal
> legend before all is said and done you will be

tested with all the lessons and conditions you have
learned and endured from beginning until now.
Know that is true and be at peace.[263]

Colin meditated again, spending a few minutes to find peace.
Then he went out once more into the storm. He managed to ski
twenty miles that day, in spite of the accident, the wind, the snow,
and the sastrugi.

The next day, still in the chaos of the storm, Colin skied a new personal best: 33.1 miles.

The storm raged for another four days until it finally broke on Day
51. When he could see the horizon once again, Colin realized that the
edge of his world was no longer flat. In the distance, the jagged ridges

On the polar plateau, there's nothing to see on the horizon except ice. [Carl Alvey/ALE]

of the Transantarctic Mountains pointed to the sky. He skied twenty-four miles, ending barely one hundred miles from the finish.

The break in the weather didn't last, and the route began climbing, again. It was only a few hundred feet, hardly anything compared to the 9,000 feet he'd already climbed, but, like every challenge, the mental struggle was worse than the physical one. He knew that he'd be heading down again soon, but it felt like he was "stuck in an M.C. Echer [sic] drawing where every direction leads up, a never ending staircase."[264] Even still, through the snow, wind, and uphill battle, on Day 52 he skied another twenty-three miles.

Colin woke up on Day 53—December 25, 2018, Christmas Day—77.54 miles from the finish.

He went through his morning routine—boil water, eat breakfast, dismantle tent, pack pulk—all while a question was growing in his mind.

"People run 100 miles all the time," he thought, as the question began to grow.[265] Seventy-eight miles didn't seem so far.

What if he could finish today?

Fifty-three days into his journey. "I just locked in to this place in my mind that was like calm and collected and I was in complete silence."[266] It came without fear or struggle and surged through every moment of thought. More than that, his body coursed with a confidence, almost an excitement that seemed out of place next to his worn, tired muscles.

The feeling never faded as he clipped into his harness and began to pull.

Ten hours. Fifteen hours. Intense concentration coursed through him.

At eighteen hours of hauling, he paused. He was out of water, and he had to put up his tent in order to boil more. It was midnight according to Chilean time, but it was only 7:00 p.m. in Portland, Oregon. When Colin called home, his family was in the middle of eating Christmas dinner.

Jenna, his mom, his five older sisters, and his stepfather all congratulated him on his longest, best day yet. They thought he was calling according to his normal bedtime routine. At that point, he had skied forty miles, and they were impressed.

Then he told them he wasn't stopping. He wasn't going to sleep; he was going to pack up and start skiing again.

Immediately, they began interrogating him. Had he eaten enough calories? Was he drinking enough water? What, really, was his state of mind? Which side of the line between daring and desperation was he on?

Question after question, Colin answered them all.

He wouldn't go, he said, unless he had Jenna's full support. Later, she remembered, "We had an open and honest and smart conversation with him, and he totally delivered."[267] She gave her blessing unconditionally.

With their enthusiasm spurring him on, Colin took down his tent, packed his pulk, and headed out into the wind and cold. For the first time in days,

There's no cell phone service in Antarctica, so the unwieldly antenna on this Iridium phone is necessary for satellite calls. [Leslie Wicks/ALE]

the snow had cleared, and in place of overwhelming whiteness, he saw cliffs, mountains, sun, and glaciers. He tried to memorize everything, every sense of it down to the smallest sound of ski against ice.

> I was aware I'm going to tell this story for the rest of my life, but I told myself: you're living this right now—live it! It was just getting deep with the senses. What does it sound like when your skis scrape against the snow. What does it taste like out here? Really just try and just live the experience.[268]

Colin O'Brady crossed the finish line, an invisible ribbon marked by a single wooden pole at the edge of the landmass of Antarctica, on December 26, 2018, after thirty-two hours and thirty minutes of hauling, covering almost eighty miles of skiing.

"I did it! I did it!" he shouted into the phone when he called Jenna. All he heard was a buzz.

"Oh, is my phone not working?" he thought.[269]

Then he realized that Jenna, his mom, his stepdad, and his sisters were screaming so loudly it sounded like static.

Over thousands of miles away, Colin heard the people he loved most cheering his victory. But even in the middle of the coldest place on earth, their voices had never really left him. From those first days recovering from the burns in Thailand, their encouragement and their enthusiasm had helped him forward.

There were so many people to thank, and he began in his first, elated victory post on Instagram by calling out his wife, his expedition manager and best friend. She had done so much to support him, to tell him time and again that the impossible was possible. She was right. They both were. He had just proved it.

Eighteen miles north of the South Pole— Day 42—December 14, 2018

Coming off the high of the South Pole wasn't easy. Lou had hugged people—other people! He had spoken real conversations. He had seen buildings.

And then . . . they were gone. He was alone, again. Faced with pulling the pulk another three hundred miles.

On top of his by-now-normal pain of hauling, he had a real medical issue as well: his lips and the roof of his mouth were cracked, pus-filled, and bleeding. It was a classic Antarctic cold injury.

Eating and drinking were miserable. Even worse, every breath he took stung as the freezing air ate into his swollen flesh. Then, as he faced into the storms, the wind sped by his lips, working its way into every crack with stinging, sharp pain.

On Day 43, he ran into two Antarctic scientists doing remote field-work, and they jumped out of their truck to cheer him on. The woman asked for a picture, and, when Lou raised his mask, her jaw dropped in surprise.

"Oh, you're bleeding," she cried.

"Just a bit," Lou replied. "I've been drinking my blood all day as I've been skiing along!"[270]

He could make light of it in a quick conversation with strangers, but the pain was inescapable, and the danger was very real. During a nightly check-in call, the ALE doctor advised him on a regimen of antibiotics.

In spite of it all, Lou pulled hard. Three days out from the pole, on

Day 44, with Pink Floyd blasting in his headphones, he set a personal best at twenty-one miles.

While he skied, he tried to sort through his injury. He had begun to notice a pattern. "I noticed that my mouth didn't hurt at all during that first two-and-a-half-hour [of the day]," Lou said. "It's only after I have a break, on some of the breaks, that it seems to trigger the pain."[271] Something he ate or drank must have been aggravating it.

He began experimenting. On the first break of the day, he only drank liquids. Not a problem—there was no pain. On the next break, he ate cheese and salami. Still no problem. But then, on his third break of the day, when he finally grabbed a random handful of bits from his grazing bag, his mouth "throbbed" and he was in "agony for an hour."[272]

He had figured it out—the acid from the little gummies (pastilles, in British English) were aggravating a small cold injury and turning the original wound into "a mass of pus and blood."[273]

"So the fruit pastilles are gone!"[274] he celebrated on his blog that night. Not gone entirely, of course; calories were too precious to just discard. He couldn't waste any of the food he was hauling, but the gummies were banished until nighttime. In the warm, still air of his tent, Lou could eat them without any fear of pain or injury.

He had mended his wound just in time, because the worst weather of the expedition was headed his way. That very night, the storm began.

"All through the night," Lou wrote, "every hour, I could hear the wind building and building, and the tent going ten to the dozen."[275] By the next morning, the wind roared at fifty miles per hour.

"I knew the forecast was bad for today," he wrote. "I didn't realize how bad it was going to be." Had it been earlier in the trip, he might have stayed in his tent all day. Even as late in the journey as it was, he "was in two minds whether or not to go for it."[276] But he, too, was getting low on food. Any progress was better than no progress at all.

It was whiteout conditions once again. The onslaught of wind churned the ground snow into a blur of spindrift, covering anything that had the audacity to be still. By the time Lou had carefully undone his campsite, the pulk was thick with snow, adding weight to the load. Lou himself was covered any time he stopped.

So, on he went.

The temperature stood at -13°F, and the wind chill took it down to almost -58°F, "just absolutely freezing cold," Lou wrote on his blog. He started skiing through breaks, just to avoid standing for even a moment.

He had barely had anything to eat—or worse, to drink—all day. Twelve hours after he started out, when he would normally end his day, "it was still howling." Stopping seemed more dangerous than keeping on. "I thought I'd go a bit longer just to see if I could get a lull so I could put the tent up," Lou explained.[277]

In bad weather, Colin and Lou had to spend all day looking down at a chest compass like this one to ensure they stayed on course. [Dylan Taylor/ALE]

But thirteen hours into his day, even as the full-force gale screamed around him, he had to stop. The storm wasn't letting up. He had to eat and drink.

Lou's tent was his lifeline. It meant heat, food, water, and rest. If anything happened to the tent, his expedition would be immediately over; his only hope would be an emergency rescue.

As the winds pounded him as hard as they had all day, Lou knew what was at risk. "If you rip the tent apart here, or even worse, lose control," Lou wrote, "you're instantly into a life-threatening situation in these conditions."[278] Before he even dared to remove the tent from its place, he "had to carabiner it onto the pulk," anchoring the tent to the heavy sled as the wind threatened to snatch it from his hand like a kite torn from a string.

Slowly, carefully, he put the tent together, lying down on it to keep it in one place as he fit the poles into their sleeves. Being "really methodical," relying on the experience he had won through thousands of miles across Antarctica, he finally managed to raise his temporary home and transfer his gear inside.[279]

It came as a total surprise when he finally had a chance to look at his GPS. He had managed twenty-three miles. It was a new personal record. "Great considering the conditions," Lou said in his voicemail to Wendy that night, the plain words masking the joy in his voice.[280]

He was so pleased with his day overall that he continued on in his voicemail and added another detail of his day. The first time he had blogged about how he "poo'ed" it had been so popular that he decided to give everyone an update: "On days like today when it's absolutely howling . . . I actually went for a poo in the vestibule of the tent . . . Which is absolutely fantastic. I only do it on rough weather days. Please don't tell anyone, it's my personal secret . . . as long as you back-fill it straightaway with a bit of snow, all isn't too bad, and it saves me going outside in 50-mile-an-hour winds and exposing my undercarriage, which would be a most unpleasant start to the day."[281]

It was bitter weather, and the conditions were not about to change. Storms earlier in the expedition had lasted a day or two at most. This one did not let up. The next day was no better, and neither was the day after that. For four days, the wind raged and snow blew so that the flat horizon was lifted to a wall of white, inches from his face.

The wind made everything bitterly cold, and Lou felt every stinging degree of temperature drop. He had lost so much body fat that all of his natural insulation was gone. It took him nearly half an hour to warm up from even a short six- or seven-minute break. At night, he sewed tucks into his thermal underwear. "I reckon I've lost four to five inches at least off my waist now, and they just kept slipping down," Lou said. "So I had to do a bit of sewing so they stay up."[282]

When the wind broke on Day 50 and he could focus on something beside the cold, he began to dream about food, "fresh food . . . a bit of bread and all those kinds of things I'm really missing."[283] It had been almost two months since his last meal that wasn't freeze-dried.

But somehow, through the hunger, pain, and solitude, he still skied on.

And then, on Day 51, all thought of misery disappeared. The sky cleared, and he began to stare at a "low cloud on the horizon . . . which looked slightly unusual. Gazing at that [as] I was skiing along . . . it suddenly dawned on me that I wasn't looking at a cloud at all, and it was actually the peak of a mountain." It was the end of the plateau, and the beginning of his steep descent. The finish was at the bottom of the mountains. It was "a hugely emotional moment" to see the rock break through and the earth reach for the sky.[284]

It was Henry Worsley now that dominated his thoughts. It was Henry now that spurred him on. Through more than seven hundred miles of Antarctic wilderness, Lou had kept Henry's crest safe. "It's really important to me that, this time, the flag goes all the way, and completes the journey right to the end," Lou wrote. "And it will."[285]

He had been getting closer to the finish every step since the start, but now Lou began to feel it as the horizon changed daily. The mountains marked "the beginning of the end," he said.[286]

Lou knew that Colin was ahead of him. They hadn't passed each other since that time so long ago on Day 6, and it came as no surprise when he received a text from Wendy on the morning of Day 54. Colin had finished. In his blog post that night, Lou congratulated his friend heartily, saying, "Fantastic. Well done to him."[287]

The Transantarctic Mountains finally broke the horizon after weeks of flat ice.
[DLR German Aerospace Center/Wikimedia Commons]

Lou was earnest in his praise. That night, during his call home, he said, "For me, I've never felt like I've been in a race. I've never been in race mode."[288] He had followed an expedition plan that was entirely his own, not dictated by anyone else. It had always been about the journey, and making sure Henry's crest made it the final way.

The day after Colin finished, Day 55, Lou set a personal best for skiing on any of his expeditions: thirty-four miles in fourteen hours of skiing. With only twenty miles to go, he would almost certainly finish the next day. With the end so near, he simply tried to take it all in. Lou had been on three Antarctic expeditions—there was no guarantee that he would ever return.

At 3:21 p.m., Chilean time, on December 28, 2018—Day 56—Lou drew even with the lone wooden stake that marked the edge of the Antarctica landmass at the base of the Leverett Glacier. He had become the first Englishman to traverse Antarctica unaided, unsupported, and solo.

In his blog post that night, Lou simply announced that he had finished and immediately began to thank those at home without whom he could not even have begun, starting with his wife and children. He thanked Wendy Searle, his expedition manager, next.

Then, Lou thanked Henry's widow and children, saying that "hopefully I've done you and Henry proud, with what I've achieved and got the flag to the far side."[289]

Finally, some piece of Henry had seen the finish.

"The goal was reached, the journey ended. I cannot say—though I know it would sound much more effective—that the object of my life was attained. That would be romancing rather too bare-facedly. I had better be honest and admit straight out that I have never known any man to be placed in such a diametrically opposite position to the goal of his desires as I was at that moment. The regions around the North Pole—well, yes, the North Pole itself—had attracted me from childhood, and here I was at the South Pole. Can anything more topsy-turvy be imagined?"

~Roald Amundsen, 1912 [290]

"We are weak, writing is difficult, but for my own sake I do not regret this journey . . . Had we lived, I should have had a tale to tell of the hardihood, endurance, and courage of my companions which would have stirred the heart of every Englishman."

~Captain Scott, "Message to the Public,"

approx. March 24, 1911 [291]

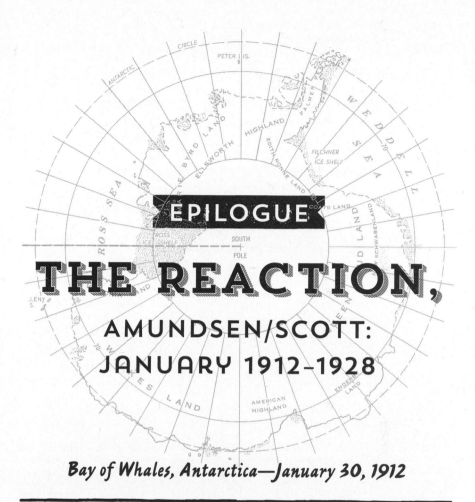

THE REACTION,

AMUNDSEN/SCOTT:
JANUARY 1912–1928

Bay of Whales, Antarctica—January 30, 1912

Amundsen and his men barely packed, taking only their most expensive equipment and their remaining, faithful dogs. The *Fram* had been waiting for them, and five days after the polar team had returned to Framheim, the entire expedition left it for good.

They hurried away, eager to head northward "on the way to that world which . . . would soon begin to expect news from us." And yet, they couldn't help feeling a bit forlorn as they said goodbye to Framheim, "a thoroughly good and comfortable home it was," wrote Amundsen.[292]

Back again at sea after 381 days in Antarctica, they sailed toward New Zealand. Amundsen locked himself in his cabin, reading through his journals and furiously writing an account of the first trip to the South Pole. News of his victory would only break once, and he had to be ready with his story before any reporter could steal the scoop.

Leon, Amundsen's trusted brother, had worked to sell the story's rights while Amundsen was away. Their hope was that an exclusive, first account of the journey would be worth a large sum of money. Victory or not, Amundsen was faced with repaying crushing debt on his return.

The freshly bathed and cleanly dressed crew of the Fram *on their arrival in Hobart, Australia. Amundsen is third from the left in the middle, seated row.*
[National Library of Norway]

At sea, the men fought storms and gigantic icebergs while Amundsen grappled with words. It was as difficult of a voyage back north as the voyage south had been easy, almost as if Antarctica hated to see them leave.

Finally, on March 4, 1912, they sighted land, and, three days later, a local navigator pulled alongside the *Fram* and offered to guide them in to Hobart, New Zealand. "One positively started at the sound of the first new human voice," Amundsen recalled.[293] It was the first time Amundsen had talked with anyone outside of his small crew in over a year.

Just like on the *Gjøa*, returning from the Northwest Passage, Amundsen and the men rushed to change into clothes they had put aside for this very moment. Scissors and razors came out as hair and beards were trimmed. Even the cook, who had been the dirtiest, smelliest man in camp at Framheim, "showed unmistakable signs of having been in close contact with water," Amundsen said.[294] In their fresh outfits, which had laid for a year in storage, they hardly looked like explorers.

Yet, by design, there were no crowds to meet them as they put into port. Amundsen had carefully laid rumors the previous year that he would sail for Lyttleton on his return. He wanted the sneaky reporters far away until he could submit his exclusive report and reap the payday.

Quietly, Amundsen sent out three telegrams, just as his brother Leon had done at the beginning of the expedition. This time, in addition to King Haakon and to his mentor, a third message went to Leon, not Scott. Quickly, and just as quietly, Leon cabled back: send the story to either side of the Atlantic—the *New York Times* in America and the *London Chronicle* in Europe.

The news broke, and the roar began.

Politicians, reporters, and celebrities all wanted to speak to the hero. Leon began arranging speaking tours and publication contracts for his brother's eventual book, playing each offer off the other and raising money with each move. Even Shackleton, now back in London, began giving quotes and offering to help with the overwhelming onslaught of interest.

Headlines ran thick and furious. As early as March 7, the *New York Times* had reported that the *Fram* had been sighted in Hobart, though they admitted that no word from the ship had reached land. Now that there was real, concrete news, reporters wouldn't let Amundsen out of their sight. Amundsen's account of the *Fram* expedition ran on Saturday, March 9, 1912. In the *New York Times*, it was the headline of the day: "Capt. Amundsen's Full Story of his Dash to the South Pole with Four of His Men and 18 Dogs."[295]

All of this excitement was a far cry from the silence that surrounded five men when they planted the victory flag at the South Pole. The secret had held and the story had broken as Amundsen wanted it to. His strategy had depended on the inability to communicate.

Yet secrecy and silence can work both for destruction as well as triumph.

In boxed text just under Amundsen's headline, another, smaller article began with terse words: "Amundsen Knows Nothing of Scott."[296]

Back on the Barrier, without any way to communicate, rescue was impossible. No one knew that as Amundsen celebrated, Scott was perishing on the ice. Amundsen had used the absence of a radio to his advantage; silence simply doomed Scott to the dark.

Cape Evans, Antarctica—March 1912

At Cape Evans, life went on as usual during the polar summer of 1911–1912. The *Terra Nova* returned to the bay once again and small sled teams left on other, planned journeys. And in early March, as Scott, Dr. Wilson, Oates, and Bowers mourned the death of Edgar Evans and fought to cover the remaining distance to the refuge at One Ton Depot—less than one hundred miles—Cherry-Garrard and the assistant dog handler, Dimitri, took a team of dogs to resupply this same spot.

Cherry-Garrard was dangerously weak and Dimitri was sick with a mysterious illness when they arrived at One Ton and faced two sets of conflicting instructions. Before he left for the pole, Scott had said to resupply One Ton but conserve the dogs as much as possible. But then, a second set of garbled instructions from Scott—relayed by the last return team of Teddy Evans, Lashly, and Crean—seemed to say to take the dogs farther south to 82° or 83°. The only way to go farther south was to begin killing dogs to be used as food, contradicting Scott's earlier instructions.

Feeble Dimitri was not able to go beyond One Ton Depot; if he went, Cherry-Garrard would have to go alone. Cherry-Garrard had to decide: How far would he go?

Wisely, he chose to stay at the depot. It would have been a huge risk for Cherry-Garrard to travel alone, and he had no news that a search and rescue was needed.

They camped for a week, searching for any sign of Scott before turning back to Cape Evans. They barely made it to camp before Cherry-Garrard collapsed.

One Ton Depot was full—they had done their duty. Yet when Cherry-Garrard and Dimitri were at One Ton, Scott had been only sixty miles away. Had Cherry-Garrard decided to head south to 82°, he almost certainly would have found Scott's party. Later, when he realized their positions, the implications of his decision would haunt him for the rest of his life.

But, in 1912, all that the Cape Evans men could do was wait and watch the horizon. They expected Scott by the end of March.

By mid-April, they stopped looking for his return.

The search party—it was never called a rescue party—left in November when the polar winter once again faded to polar summer. On November 12, 1912, just south and west of One Ton Depot, they saw the top of Scott's tent sticking out above a drift. "To say it has been a ghastly day cannot express it," Cherry-Garrard wrote in his journal.[297]

Apsley Cherry-Garrard. Decades later, he wrote a book, The Worst Journey in the World, *about his experience on the* Terra Nova *expedition. [Herbert Ponting/ Wikimedia Commons]*

They had not died easy deaths. Their bodies were scarred, yellow, and frozen. The syringe was still full of morphine, and all the opium tablets were accounted for. They had not committed suicide to lessen their pain. Seeing the scene, Cherry-Garrard wrote that "we never realized how strong that man [Scott] was, mentally and physically, until now."[298]

Letters were scattered on the floor, and Scott's journal lay tucked under his arm. The search party combed the tent for personal items to return to the next of kin. Gran, the Norwegian ski master, had stayed outside the tent as a mark of respect to a different nationality. He jumped when a loud crack rang out in the silence. Inside, they had broken Scott's frozen arm to get to his journal.

The men had known that their search was for death. They had no illusions of a miracle. But their grief was tremendous. On reading Scott's journal, Cherry-Garrard recorded that they "learnt that Amundsen had been to the Pole, and that they [Scott's team] too had been to the Pole, and both items of news seemed to be of no importance whatever."[299] No one cared about such things in the face of tragedy.

In place of a burial, they lowered the tent over the bodies and raised a twelve-foot cairn as a monument. Together, they sang Scott's favorite hymn, "Onward Christian Soldiers," and read a chapter from the Bible.

From Scott's journal, they learned how Oates had died. A few men skied on for several miles, but they never found his body. When they turned back to Cape Evans, Gran wore Scott's skis, determined that they should finish the journey their master never would.

The *Terra Nova* returned to Cape Evans in early 1913, and the last of Scott's men began to make their way home. In Timaru, New Zealand, they sent messages to each of the five men's families and to the Central News Agency in London. There was finally resolution to the race to the bottom of the earth.

Scott's death stunned the world. At St. Paul's cathedral in London, a public memorial service drew a bigger crowd than the one the year before, held in memory of the victims on the *Titanic*.

When Amundsen heard that Scott had died, he refused to believe it. The press often got things wrong—at one point or another, the media

Fossils, like these trace fossils found at the modern-day ALE Union Glacier camp, were important scientific finds brought back by Scott's team. [David Hamilton/ALE]

had reported that both he and Shackleton had died as well.

But, when he did finally come to know the truth, he praised Scott as a brave man who thought of others before he thought of himself. He wrote that "nobody could hold a higher admiration than myself for the gallant courage of our brave English competitors, for nobody else so well as we can understand the fearful dangers of the trip."[300]

Underestimating those dangers had cost Scott and four other men their lives. Courageous though he might have been, Scott's litany of mistakes—underestimating the weather, secretive and authoritative planning, poor understanding of polar travel, a mistrust of dogs, and a failure to retreat—had fatal consequences, not only for himself but also for those who followed his lead.

Scott went into an unknown world without the humility to understand his own weaknesses. Failure was almost inevitable.

Yet in the years after his death, Scott's journey was held as a point of national pride. He had reached the pole and had done so by the "pure" form of man-hauling. Then, when the end had finally come, he had held out to the last, refusing to ease his departure at all with opium. Whatever else his actions meant, none had ever shown he was a weak man.

Cherry-Garrard wrote his own account of the *Terra Nova* expedition in the book *The Worst Journey in the World*. In it, he asked the question that surely crossed Scott's mind: "Is life worth risking for a feat, or losing for your country?" Cherry-Garrard answered as he knew Scott must have: "To face a thing because it was a feat, and only a feat, was not very attractive to Scott: it had to contain an additional object—knowledge."[301]

Scott had not been the first to the pole, but exploration had never been his only goal. Science—research and discovery—were as integral to his journey to the pole as it was to be the first. The goal of bringing back new information about the natural world rang true throughout even his toughest days.

Amundsen's legacy was just as complicated as his rival's. He had achieved a great victory for the newly independent Norway by reaching the pole first and by returning with all of his men. But, there was something almost underhanded about the way he had done it, turning Scott's expedition into a race between two groups. And, of course, his journey had held almost no scientific value.

To Amundsen, the point of Scott's voyage was for science, with the pole as only a "side-issue"; for his own expedition, those goals were directly reversed. Amundsen argued that he had sent Scott the telegram announcing his own expedition to the South Pole "rather as a mark of courtesy than as a communication which might cause him to

A photo of penguins, taken by one of the men of the Fram *expedition.*
[National Library of Norway]

alter his programme in the slightest degree."[302] It was a friendly message, not the shotgun at the beginning of a race.

Yet whatever his words might say, Amundsen's every action indicated that he was clearly in a race and wholeheartedly intent on beating Scott.

Amundsen had worked for years to ensure his victory. His decades spent in polar environments led him to an instinctive feel for what was needed in the unknown. No one told him to, but before he left Norway, Amundsen had his fuel tins soldered shut, above and beyond what came from the supplier. Though his food on the Barrier rotted the same as Scott's, Amundsen never faced shortages of fuel. He simply had the foresight to understand where weaknesses lay.

Amundsen's excess of knowledge and experience ensured his survival. These were lessons that were gleaned over many years, the result of polar exploration as a well-defined, lifelong pursuit.

After returning home, Amundsen never saw the South Pole again, but he set many records in the north. His major expeditions after the South Pole included the first sea voyage through the Northeast Passage, using a plane to fly over the Arctic, and crossing the Arctic (possibly even the North Pole) in an airship. Many times, men from his South Pole expedition accompanied him. Wisting and Hanssen, especially, were eager to join him again and again.

In the end, Amundsen wasn't to die a quiet death, either. He had long used his polar expertise to assist those in danger, and when an Italian explorer became stranded in the Arctic ice, Amundsen was one of the first to volunteer for the rescue mission.

He took off on a Latham biplane with several French and Norwegian crew members on June 18, 1928. The overloaded, underpowered plane lost radio contact soon after takeoff. Fifty-five-year-old Amundsen perished along with the rest. Perhaps, to an explorer, there could be no death more honorable.

The victory at the South Pole clearly belonged to Amundsen, not Scott. But over the following century, popular consensus turned and turned again to vilify, then laud, first one and then the other. Amundsen lived to tell and craft his tale with the talent of a born optimist and storyteller; Scott was given the golden aura of martyrdom.

Most telling is that both men had loyal, faithful followers to the very end.

Roald Amundsen (1923). [Wikimedia Commons]

"This has been one of the most profound and meaningful experiences of my entire life, and without a doubt my proudest accomplishment."

~Colin O'Brady, December 30, 2018 [303]

"But what we have done is show what is possible and opened the door for future unsupported traverses of the continent. If what I've done with this expedition inspires just one person to pursue their goals or overcome a difficult challenge then I'll be happy."

~Lou Rudd, January 14, 2019 [304]

THE REACTION,

O'BRADY/RUDD:
DECEMBER 28, 2018–
NOVEMBER 2019

Base of the Leverett Glacier, Antarctica—
Day 56—December 28, 2018

It was "a minor miracle that both of us have completed" the journey, Lou said, and it was a happy day for Colin when Lou arrived.[305]

Colin was out of food.

He had stretched his rations to the bare minimum, and two days after arriving at the finish, "my personal food was more or less gone," Colin recalled.[306] In 2017, ALE had buried a celebration package for Ben Saunders, and the bundle of treats had stayed frozen in the ice at the finish line after Ben had ended his journey at the South Pole.

Colin dug up the stash and ate the waiting chocolate, cheese, and ham (and found the note that said "Congratulations, Ben!").[307] Then, when he arrived, Lou good-naturedly shared his extra food, never having reduced his calories along the way.

Though Lou was "half expecting a Twin Otter to be there waiting" when he arrived at the finish, thick fog in Union Glacier meant that the ALE plane couldn't leave.[308] Colin and Lou were still trapped on the ice. After almost two months and more than nine hundred miles, it was frustrating to be done and still so far from comfort.

Finally, on December 31—Day 59—two days after Lou arrived and a long four days after Colin had first reached the finish, the plane "popped through the clouds and landed next to our camp at the Ross Ice Shelf," Colin wrote.[309] ALE friends with huge grins and celebratory champagne helped them load the pulks. Their solo journeys had ended, and they left their expeditions as they had begun, together on a plane.

They arrived back in Union Glacier at midnight, and in spite of the late hour, a crowd gathered to cheer their arrival. Everyone wanted to congratulate and hug the men—that is, after they took showers. Neither Colin nor Lou had bathed in almost two months. Their smell was unbearable.

The Twin Otter with skis as landing gear. [Adam Ungar/ALE]

Hot-water showers. Fresh food. Heat. Conversation. After nearly sixty days hauling hundreds of pounds through some of the worst weather in the world, it seemed like the height of luxury. And yet . . .

Lou called the finish line an "anti-climax."[310] The pain was behind them, but so too was the adventure. It was time to be done, but the end left them with its own kind of ache as well.

There was an "underlying sadness that the adventure is drawing to a close," Colin wrote.[311] After all, how do you explain a journey that only one other person on the planet has also experienced?

While hauling, there had been an almost ascetic solitude, but now the difference they felt around other people—the separation, the "otherness"—was just as hard. Beginning their re-entrance to the world of people was easier at Union Glacier; at least here everyone spoke with the same passion for Antarctica.

They spent a few days recovering, eating, relaxing, and adjusting.

Riding a fat-tire bike at the Union Glacier base camp was a relaxing way to spend time after hauling for nearly two months. [Eric Larsen/ALE]

The Ilyushin aircraft, which took Colin and Lou back to Punta Arenas, Chile after their expeditions, against the background of mountains at the Union Glacier base camp. [Adam Ungar/ALE]

But, when the weather cleared enough to fly once again, they left. The giant Ilyushin plane carried them off the blue ice runway, and they glimpsed their last of the ice.

Colin reunited with his wife, and, together, they flew to Standard Process's research facilities in North Carolina. Everyone was amazed that he had lost only twenty pounds. Personalized nutrition, to the extent that Colin had used it, was enormously expensive and time-consuming. But, clearly, it worked. Soon, Colin was in New York City being interviewed on the *Today Show*, and long lists of media interviews and accolades followed.

Lou, too, didn't get to go home right away. He went to NYC as well, and was interviewed on *CBS This Morning* and at the headquarters of the *New York Times*. He was made a member, like Roald Amundsen and Colin, of the famous Explorers Club. Eventually, he flew back to the UK and was reunited with his family on January 9, 2019.

They each came home to a hero's welcome. Their stories were featured with headlines in some of the most important news outlets, and their fans cheered their successes. The *New York Times* ran a set of eight articles about the race, and *National Geographic* featured both of their journeys.

"I've been staggered by the amount of media interest it's generated," Lou wrote.[312] Polar exploration was news like it hadn't been in over a hundred years.

But not everyone was impressed. Within the triumph of their return ran a sliver of controversy. They had called themselves the first to traverse Antarctica unassisted, unsupported, and solo. Many people started calling them liars.

More people were paying attention to Antarctica, and now more people knew the name Borge Ousland. Over the polar summer of 1996–1997, Borge had traveled from the edge of the Ronne Ice Shelf to the far edge of the Ross Ice Shelf—1,864 miles to Lou's and Colin's 925 miles—and he had done it alone and without resupplies. He had been aided; he had used a kite to manage more than 100 miles a day. But, if someone was going to claim a traverse of Antarctica, wasn't his route the one to use?

And then, people began to question how "unsupported" Lou and Colin's journeys were, really. After all, they had daily check-ins with ALE, and Colin talked to his wife every night. He later said that "she gave me words of encouragement to keep me on track and moving forward every single day. There's no way I could have done [the expedition] without it."[313] And when Lou's mouth was a mess, he spoke to a doctor who prescribed medication. Both were examples of support, weren't they?

The SPOT road came under examination, too. Though neither mentioned much about it, from the South Pole to the finish, they had followed the South Pole Overland Traverse road. The crevasses were filled in and markers were planted every 100 meters, keeping them on route. Didn't those help as well?

For Lou, the condemnation hurt. The armchair quarterbacks could be forgiven their ignorance, but it was deeply mystifying how the small, normally supportive community of polar explorers could seemingly turn on them.

The SPOT road, which Colin and Lou followed from the South Pole to the base of the Leverett Glacier, was designed to facilitate caravans like this one, moving supplies between the US research stations at McMurdo Sound and the South Pole.

Lou had never sought headline media attention. "Yes, it would have been nice to finish first," he conceded, but, for him, the title had always been secondary.[314] Lou was adamant: "It's all about the journey."[315]

When the media got hold of his story, Lou's message had been buried under the hype of a race. Antarctica mattered. The journey mattered. Remembering Henry mattered. For Lou, turning it all into a race at the last moment barely registered. And now the attention was generating controversy on top of it. It knocked him down twice—first the mangling of his message and now the negativity about his journey.

The "churned up heavily rutted surface" that Lou references is clearly visible.
[Peter Rejcek, US Antarctic Program/Wikimedia Commons]

After their return, Lou began using the term "traverse of the Antarctic landmass" more often to describe the expedition. Perhaps the clarification was helpful, and it was the truth. If adding "landmass" cleared the air, then so be it.

As for the SPOT road, according to Lou, "it's a churned up heavily rutted surface that is mostly buried in soft spindrift. . . . actually skiing parallel to the road on the much firmer flanks was mostly a better option." Then to anyone questioning the markers, he easily dismissed their concerns, noting that "having successfully navigated over 2,500 miles across Antarctica previously without them, I don't think they were a deal breaker!"[316]

The real advantage of the SPOT road was how carefully crevasses were monitored. And there, he had always been blunt: he was a father and a husband. Safety came first.

Lou had accomplished a great goal and honored a mentor and friend. The minor detractions leveled at him seemed less focused on his journey and Antarctica than on the 24/7 news cycle and generating hype. The controversy—like the race itself—made for good headlines, but it was hardly the full truth.

While Lou grappled with the un-sought-after attention, Colin came under even more intense scrutiny. His loud, boasting claims of the "Impossible First" drew criticism with headlines like "Fake News: Cheating at the South Pole" and "O'Brady's Antarctic Crossing: Was It Really Unassisted?" Even the *New York Times*, which had been so flattering earlier, published an op-ed, explaining how Borge's record outshone Colin's. Borge himself went so far as to say that Colin's journey was "not impossible, and it's not the first."[317]

In a later exposé of his journey, *National Geographic* quoted leading polar explorers as saying that Colin "has distorted the truth in pursuit of fame." He had a successful expedition, no one argued that.

The trouble was his self-imposed labels driven by a desire to be a celebrity, not a polar explorer. It looked to many like he had taken an easy way out; he had anointed himself a hero where he had not done work worthy of the title.

While Colin, like Lou, began using the term "landmass" in association with the expedition, he defended his journey. Though Colin said that Borge's traverse was "exceptionally inspirational to me,"[318] he maintained that the two traverses were "like comparing apples and oranges . . . it's like the difference between sailing a boat across the ocean and rowing a boat across an ocean."[319] In Colin's mind, Borge's record and his own were compatible and both "firsts," just in very different ways.

To the rest of the criticism, "I just smile and move on," Colin said.[320]

The record—the solo, unaided, unsupported traverse—was a debate without a clear-cut answer, and one that would never come. It all depended on how the terms were defined and who defined them. After all, didn't twenty-first-century skis offer assistance over those from 1911, and weren't Colin Bars a better source of nutrition than pemmican? The pulks used by Colin and Lou were many times lighter than the sleds used by Amundsen and Scott—was that a form of assistance? Where, exactly, was the line drawn?

The simple truth was that Colin and Lou had completed an incredible expedition, a huge feat of monumental effort.

Colin's ultramarathon of almost eighty miles, too, was remarkable. After his expedition, Lou graciously said that even he "probably couldn't do that . . . especially at that stage right at the end. If my life depended on it, maybe, but I wouldn't choose to do it. Hats off to him. He's an extreme performance athlete."[321] Records and firsts could and would be disputed, but there was no doubt that the expeditions were extraordinary.

That someone would someday surpass their record—time, distance, alternate route—they both acknowledged and encouraged. "It's just a matter of time," Lou said.[322] Theirs were simply firsts, not absolutes. It was up to the next generation to make the next records greater.

Colin had always wanted to use his victory to inspire others. On coming back to the US, he became a sought-after motivational speaker, and he was inundated with some one thousand appearance requests in the first months after his return. He spoke to Fortune 500 companies and addressed high school commencement ceremonies, sometimes charging five-figure fees for his speeches.

To everyone, he spoke about the universal truth that greatness happens outside of your comfort zone. That he would break out and push his own boundaries again was certain. On November 15, 2019, he announced his next project: attempting to row across the Drake Passage as part of the first fully human-powered crossing. But, like

Lou Rudd and Colin O'Brady on their return flight from Union Glacier to Punta Arenas— competitors and friends. [TAMARA MERINO/New York Times/Redux]

the Impossible First, he waited until just before launch to share the adventure. After all, breaking and setting records for a living demanded a careful strategy; he couldn't tell just anyone his dreams.

Lou, too, spoke extensively. He spent five months visiting schools and scouting groups around the UK, all for free. Lou was not a professional athlete; crossing Antarctica was merely "a hobby," as he called it.[323] He was still on active military duty, and he returned to his job.

In November 2019—one year after he began his own journey—he repaid the favor that Wendy, his expedition manager, had shown him: he became her expedition manager as she attempted to break a speed record for hauling to the South Pole. No matter what else the future might hold, Lou was certain that he would continue to help the next generation plan, prepare, and train for their own polar adventures, just as previous generations had taught him.

It had all gone back and back and back. Explorers of all kinds passed on their knowledge and passion, helping the next generation to go farther. Lou had learned from Henry Worsley, and Henry Worsley had Antarctica in his blood—his ancestor Frank Worsley had been the captain of Shackleton's Antarctic ship *Endurance*. In one long, continuing story of expedition and adventure in Antarctica, even Shackleton and Scott were still teaching explorers today.

Someone had once calculated that if Scott had taken just eleven extra steps every day during his tragic South Pole journey, he would have successfully reached One Ton Depot with its safety and refuge.

Lou was not a superstitious man, but there was one tradition that he held to be sacred. At the end of each day, he would decide to stop, plant his ski poles in the ice, and come to a halt.

Then he would take eleven more steps.

It was a motto he lived by: "Onwards."[324]

SKIP TO THE END FOR A SNEAK PEEK OF...

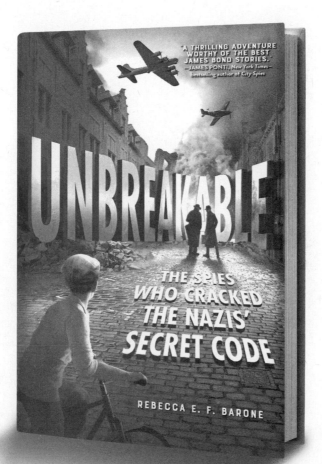

ACKNOWLEDGMENTS

This story would have been much different had it not been for Brian Geffen's amazing vision, insight, and encouragement in editing and shepherding it along. We may have different ideas about the ideal temperature for a vacation, but this adventure story found the perfect home at his desk. To the rest of the team at HBFYR—Liz Dresner, Kay Petronio, Jie Yang, Ilana Worrell, Judy Kiviat, Lelia Mander, Kelsey Marrujo, and Cassandra Gutman—thank you for turning my manuscript into this beautiful book.

Michael Bourret's enthusiasm for this project lit the way forward from the start, and I owe him many thanks for his endless patience in answering round after round of questions (and nonfiction authors can have a *lot* of questions!) and the reassurance he's given at every step of the way.

I am deeply indebted to Antarctica Logistics and Expeditions for their help. Leslie Wicks first put me in contact with Steve Jones, who graciously spent hours explaining and recounting details of how expeditions are planned and executed. Liz Galloway was invaluable with her media help and wonderfully tenacious in getting the technology to work correctly! This book would have been a much weaker report without them.

The research for this book was daunting in many ways, and I'm grateful to Adrienne McChesney, Aaron Teasdale, Hilary Bureck, and Rebecka Churchill for their help in understanding concepts and pinning down details.

It was a lucky day for me when Andrew Speno replied and then introduced me to Tracy Vonder Brink. I cannot thank both of them enough for the hours and hours they spent reading and reviewing and for their friendship. I'm also especially thankful for the critiques from Olga Frimenko, Katie Van Oss, and Heather Weis.

I never would have started writing nonfiction if it hadn't been for Rebecca Morris, and there are many times I would have stopped had it not been for her—thank you, dear friend!

To my parents, Danielle and Jacob, who put a poster of Rosie the Riveter next to the icons of saints—

To my sisters, Nika, Hilary, and Katya, who know all the quotes—

To Adam and Lydia, who are in every page of this book—

To Dominic, whose faith carried me through—

Thank you

BIBLIOGRAPHY

"1st Explorer to Trek Antarctica Solo and Unassisted Shares Story." *TODAY.com.* Accessed March 20, 2019. *https://www.today.com /video/1st-explorer-to-trek-antarctica-solo-and-unassisted-shares -story-1423322691608.*

"10 Things to Know about the Ilyushin IL-76 TD | ALE." *Antarctic Logistics & Expeditions*, April 13, 2016, *https://antarctic-logistics .com/2016/04/13/10-things-to-know-about-the-ilyushin-76td/.*

"A Pioneer's Pulk (Lou Rudd Interview)." *Shackleton London.* Accessed February 26, 2019. *https://shackletonlondon.com/blogs/blog/a -pioneer-s-pulk-what-did-lou-rudd-haul-across-antarctica.*

All About Sea Ice | National Snow and Ice Data Center. Accessed March 14, 2019. *https://nsidc.org/cryosphere/seaice/index.html.*

Allen, Andrew, and Jack Hudson. "Chasing Shackleton." *Shackleton London*, October 3, 2018, *https://shackletonlondon.com/blogs/pre-expedition /chasing-shackleton.*

Amundsen, Roald. "Crosses Ice Barrier and Reaches the Goal in Fifty-Five Days.; AT POLE DEC. 14, 3 P.M." *The New York Times*, March 9, 1912, 1–3.

—. *My Life as an Explorer.* 1st ed., Doubleday, Page & Company, 1927.

—. *The South Pole: An Account of the Norwegian Antarctic Expedition in the "Fram," 1910–1912.* Pantianos Classics, 1913.

—. *To the North Magnetic Pole and Through the Northwest Passage.* Shorey's Bookstore, 1967.

"AntarcticDEM Explorer." *ESRI.* Accessed December 19, 2019. *https://livingat las2.arcgis.com/antarcticdemexplorer/.*

Baker. "Amundsen Knows Nothing of Scott." *New York Times*, March 9, 1912, p. 1.

BBC—History—Scott of the Antarctic. Accessed December 1, 2018. *http:// www.bbc.co.uk/history/historic_figures/scott_of_antarctic.shtml.*

Beresini, Erin. "Colin O'Brady Profile and Feature from the Fall 2016 *USA Triathlon Magazine*." *Team USA.* Accessed September 9, 2019. *https:// www.teamusa.org:443/USA-Triathlon/About/USAT/Magazine /Colin-OBrady-Fall-2016.*

"Borchgrevink Hut Cape Adare." *Antarctic Heritage.* Accessed February 28, 2019. *https://www.nzaht.org/explorer-bases/borchgrevink-hut-cape-adare.*

Brangham, William. "How Colin O'Brady Mentally Prepared for His Antarctic Feat." *PBS NewsHour*, January 17, 2019. *https://www.pbs.org/newshour /show/how-colin-obrady-mentally-prepared-for-his-antarctic-feat.*

Braun, Davey. "Alone Across Antarctica Part 1: Unbreakable Colin O'Brady Achieves the Impossible Once Again." *The Outdoor Journal*, July 10, 2019. *https://www.outdoorjournal.com/featured/unbreakable-colin -obrady-antarctica-world-record/.*

—. "Alone Across Antarctica Part 2: Captain Louis Rudd—For the Love of the Journey." *The Outdoor Journal*, July 15, 2019. *https://www.outdoorjour nal.com/featured/athletes-and-explorers/captain-louis-rudd-antarc tica-crossing/.*

—. "Alone Across Antarctica Part 3: Nowhere to Hide—Børge Ousland's World Record Legacy." *The Outdoor Journal*, July 17, 2019. *https://www .outdoorjournal.com/featured/athletes-and-explorers/borge-ousland -antarctica-legacy/.*

—. "Alone Across Antarctica Part 4: Mike Horn's Race Against Time." *The Outdoor Journal*, July 22, 2019. *https://www.outdoorjournal.com /featured/athletes-and-explorers/mike-horn-antarctica-record/.*

—. "Alone Across Antarctica Part 5: The Impossible Truth on Antarctica." *The Outdoor Journal*, July 25, 2019. *https://www.outdoorjournal.com /featured/athletes-and-explorers/obrady-impossible-truth-world -record-antarctica/.*

—. "Introducing Alone Across Antarctica: The Full Story and Controversy." *The Outdoor Journal*, July 8, 2019. *https://www.outdoorjournal.com /featured/alone-across-antarctica-controversy/.*

Brueck, Hilary. "The 33-year-old who just became the first person to cross Antarctica alone says 2 simple mantras were crucial to his success." *Business Insider*, January 20, 2019. *https://www.businessinsider.com /why-colin-obrady-crossed-antarctica-fire-burns-2019-1.*

—. "We Tried the 1,250-Calorie Survival Bar That Powered Colin O'Brady's Record-Shattering 932-Mile Solo Journey Across Antarctica." *Business Insider*, January 12, 2019. *https://www.businessinsider.com/colin -obrady-1250-calorie-energy-bar-antarctica-taste-test-2019-1.*

—. "Solo Trek across Antarctica: Will Colin O'Brady Be First to Survive?" *Business Insider*, 2018, *https://www.businessinsider.com/solo-trek-across -antarctica-colin-obrady-2018–11.*

"Captain Lou Rudd MBE Set to Capture the Spirit of Endurance." *The Soldiers' Charity*, October 18, 2018. *https://soldierscharity.org/captain-lou-rudd -set-to-capture-the-spirit-of-endurance/.*

CBS This Morning. *Lou Rudd on the Songs That Got Him through Solo Antarc tica Trek. YouTube.* Accessed March 5, 2019. *https://www.youtube.com /watch?v=CTqSOywdGI4.*

Cherry-Garrard, Apsley. *The Worst Journey in the World: With Scott in Antarctica 1910–1913*. Penguin Books, 2013.

Craig. "Is the BBC Biased?: Rudd of the Antarctic." *Is the BBC Biased?*, January 2, 2017. *http://isthebbcbiased.blogspot.com/2017/01/rudd-of-antarctic .html*.

Crane, David. *Scott of the Antarctic: A Life of Courage and Tragedy*. Vintage Books, 2007.

Crofts, Cassie. "How The Race to the South Pole Went Down." *National Geographic*, December 14, 2016. *https://www.nationalgeographic.com .au/history/the-race-to-the-south-pole.aspx*.

Diagram of Amundsen and Scott's Polar Expeditions. February 24, 2015, *https://bureau.ru/en/projects/amundsen-and-scott/*.

Edward Adrian Wilson (1872–1912)—Biographical Notes. Accessed May 1, 2019. *https://www.coolantarctica.com/Antarctica%20fact%20file /History/biography/Wilson-Edward-Adrian.php*.

"Expedition Overview (Spirit of Endurance)." *Shackleton London*. Accessed March 4, 2019. *https://shackletonlondon.com/blogs/lou-s-journal /spirit-of-endurance-lou-rudd-antarctic-journey*.

Fallon, Sarah. "People Cross Antarctica All the Time. It's Still Crazy Hard." *Wired*, Feb. 2016. *www.wired.com, https://www.wired.com /2016/02/people-cross-antarctica-all-the-time-its-still-crazy -hard/*.

Farley, Adam. "High Endurance." *Irish America*, August 10, 2016. *https:// irishamerica.com/2016/08/high-endurance/*.

Fiddes, Archie. "Louis Rudd Solo Traverses Antarctica." *Shackleton London*, January 8, 2019. *https://shackletonlondon.com/blogs/expedition -support-meet-our-record-breakers/spirit-of-endurance-lou-rudd -antarctic-journey*.

Fiennes, Sir Ranulph. *Race to the Pole: Tragedy, Heroism, and Scott's Antarctic Quest*. Hyperion, 2004.

Fram Museum—Fram Museum. Accessed June 3, 2019. *https://web.archive .org/web/20110724175458/http://www.frammuseum.no/Polar-Heroes /Heroes/Sverre-Hassel.aspx*.

Gade, Herman G. "Bjørn Helland-Hansen." *Norsk Biografisk Leksikon*, September 28, 2014. *Store norske leksikon, http://nbl.snl.no/Bj%C3%B8rn _Helland-Hansen*.

Gervais, Michael. "Colin O'Brady: Explorers Grand Slam | Finding Mastery Podcast." *Finding Mastery*, July 20, 2016. *https://findingmastery.net /colin-obrady/*.

Getlen, Larry. "How Colin O'Brady Crossed the World's Most Unforgiving Place in 54 Days." *New York Post*, February 22, 2020. *https://nypost*

.com/2020/02/22/how-colin-obrady-crossed-the-worlds-most
-unforgiving-place-in-54-days/.

Ghosh, Pallab. "Researchers Praise Scott's Legacy." January 17, 2012. *www
.bbc.com*, *https://www.bbc.com/news/science-environment-16530953*.

Gildea, Damien. "Crossing Antarctica: How the Confusion Began and Where
Do We Go from Here." *Explorersweb*. Accessed April 2, 2019. *https://
explorersweb.com/2019/01/09/crossing-antarctica-how-the-confusion
-began-and-where-do-we-go-from-here/*.

Gordon, Keith. "How Adventurer Colin O'Brady Became the First Man to
Cross Antarctica Solo." *Maxim*. Accessed May 7, 2019. *https://www
.maxim.com/news/colin-obrady-crosses-antarctica-2019-4*.

Graham-Harrison, Emma. "'I'm Absolutely Elated. It's a Miracle We Made It,'
Says Polar Hero Louis Rudd." *The Observer*, December 29, 2018. *www.
theguardian.com*, *https://www.theguardian.com/world/2018
/dec/29/louis-rudd-antarctic-explorer-describes-trek*.

Grann, David. *Retracing the Antarctic Journey of Henry Worsley*. October
2018. *www.newyorker.com*, *https://www.newyorker.com/news
/news-desk/retracing-the-antarctic-journey-of-henry-worsley*.

—. *The White Darkness: A Journey Across Antarctica*. February 2018. *www
.newyorker.com*, *https://www.newyorker.com/magazine/2018/02/12
/the-white-darkness*.

Hatfield, Stefano. "This Is the Side of Antarctic Explorer Henry Worsley That
the Media Shies Away From." *The Independent*, January 31, 2016. *http://
www.independent.co.uk/voices/this-is-the-side-of-antarctic-explorer
-henry-worsley-that-the-media-shies-away-from-a6845381.html*.

"History of Shackleton's Expedition." *Antarctic Heritage*. Accessed May 2,
2019. *https://www.nzaht.org/pages/history-of-shackletons-expedition*.

Hudson, Jack. "A Mind In Extremis." *Shackleton London*. Accessed March 4,
2019. *https://shackletonlondon.com/blogs/pre-expedition/a-mind-in
-extremis*.

—. "Cold Extremities (SPEAR17 Interview)." *Shackleton London*, October 25,
2018. *https://shackletonlondon.com/blogs/pre-expedition/spear-17*.

—. "Equipping a Modern Pioneer." *Shackleton London*, November 28, 2018.
https://shackletonlondon.com/blogs/pre-expedition/modern-pioneer.

—. "Lou Rudd Returns to the UK." *Shackleton*, January 10, 2019. *https://shack
letonlondon.com/blogs/lou-s-journal/lou-rudd-returns-to-the-uk*.

—. "Watchkeeper (Wendy Searle Interview)." *Shackleton*, November 20, 2018.
https://shackletonlondon.com/blogs/pre-expedition/watchkeeper.

Huntford, Roland. *Race for the South Pole: The Expedition Diaries of Scott and
Amundsen*. Continuum International Publishing Group, 2010.

Hutchinson, Alex. *Endure: Mind, Body, and the Curiously Elastic Limits of Human Performance*. HarperCollins, 2018.

—. *How to Fuel for a Solo, Unassisted Antarctic Crossing | Outside Online*. November 14, 2018. *https://www.outsideonline.com/2365661/colin -obrady-how-fuel-solo-unassisted-antarctic-crossing*.

—. "The Greatest Challenge on a Solo Antarctic Crossing? Food." *Outside Online*, November 14, 2018. *https://www.outsideonline.com/2365661 /colin-obrady-how-fuel-solo-unassisted-antarctic-crossing*.

Huxley, Elspeth Joscelin Grant. *Scott of the Antarctic*. University of Nebraska Press, 1990.

"Iceland Pre-Expedition Training (Video)." *Shackleton London*. Accessed March 4, 2019. *https://shackletonlondon.com/blogs/pre-expedition /iceland-training*.

"Into the White (Official Expedition Video)." *Shackleton*. Accessed March 4, 2019. *https://shackletonlondon.com/blogs/pre-expedition/into-the -white*.

Jones, Stephen. *Interview with Steve Jones of Antarctica Logistics & Expeditions #2*. August 9, 2019.

—. *Interview with Steve Jones of Antarctica Logistics & Expeditions*. April 2, 2019.

Kirtley, Paul. "PK Podcast 012: Lou Rudd on Unsupported Polar Journeys and Retracing Amundsen's Route to the South Pole." *Paul Kirtley's Blog*, January 7, 2016. *http://paulkirtley.co.uk/2016/lou-rudd-unsupported -polar-journeys-retracing-amundsens-route-south-pole/*.

—. "PK Podcast 034: Lou Rudd on the Motivation to Traverse Antarctica Solo, Unsupported and Unaided." *Paul Kirtley's Blog*, November 19, 2018. *https://paulkirtley.co.uk/2018/lou-rudd-on-the-motivation-to -traverse-antarctica-solo-unsupported-and-unaided/*.

Klover, Geir. "Lessons from the Northwest Passage: Roald Amundsen's Experiences in the Canadian Arctic." *Canadian Geographic*, May 31, 2017. *https://www.canadiangeographic.ca/article/lessons-northwest -passage-roald-amundsens-experiences-canadian-arctic*.

Knapton, Sarah. "British Polar Explorer Ben Saunders Echoes Shackleton as He Abandons Quest to Cross South Pole Unassisted." *The Telegraph*, December 29, 2017. *www.telegraph.co.uk*, *https://www.telegraph.co.uk /science/2017/12/29/british-polar-explorer-ben-saunders-echoes -shackleton-has-abandons/*.

Kuo, John, and Anna Helhoski. "The Cost of Extreme Sports: Pricey Gear and Life Insurance." *NerdWallet*, December 15, 2015. *https://www .nerdwallet.com/blog/insurance/life-insurance-cost-of-extreme -sports-2015/*.

Larsen, Joar Hoel. "Peder Christophersen." *Norsk Biografisk Leksikon*, September 29, 2014. *Store norske leksikon, http://nbl.snl.no/Peder _Christophersen.*

Lewis, Tim. "Walks on the White Side: Bold, Impressive . . . but What's the Point? | Tim Lewis." *The Guardian*, December 9, 2018. *www.theguard ian.com, https://www.theguardian.com/global/blog/2018/dec/09/ louis-rudd-colin-obrady-polar-expeditions.*

Llanas, Sheila Griffin. *Who Reached the South Pole First?* Capstone, 2011.

Loder, Sandy. "Into the Unknown-Extreme Leadership in the Antarctic (via Passle)." *Passle*, December 29, 2016. *http://insights.peak-dynamics .net/post/102dwmo/into-the-unknown-extreme-leadership-in-the -antarctic.*

"Lou Rudd to Begin Attempt to Traverse Antarctic Continent—the Spirit of Endurance Expedition." *The Great Outdoors*, October 24, 2018. *https:// www.tgomagazine.co.uk/news/lou-rudd-to-begin-attempt-to -traverse-antarctic-continent-the-spirit-of-endurance-expedition/.*

Martin, Colin. "Antarctica: Scientists to the End." *Nature* 481 (January 2012): 264. doi:10.1038/481264a.

McChesney, Adrienne. *Research Questions—Thank You!* May 15, 2019.

—. *Research Questions—Thank You!* May 17, 2019.

—. *Research Questions—Thank You!* May 22, 2019.

Mintz, Luke. "British Explorer Ben Saunders Abandons Historic Trek Across Antarctica." *The Independent*, December 28, 2017. *http://www.inde pendent.co.uk/news/uk/home-news/ben-saunders-trek-antarctic -abandoned-uk-explorer-a8132451.html.*

Minutaglio, Rose. "Inside Colin O'Brady's History-Making Solo Trek Across Antarctica." *Esquire*, January 24, 2019. *https://www.esquire.com/news -politics/a25922112/colin-obrady-antarctica-solo-trek-inside/.*

Murray, Carl. "The Use and Abuse of Dogs on Scott's and Amundsen's South Pole Expeditions." *Polar Record* 44, no. 4 (October 2008): 303–10. doi:10.1017/S0032247408007493.

National Institute for Fitness and Sport *BodPod*. Accessed April 7, 2019. *https://www.nifs.org/fitness-center/fitness-assessments/bodpod.*

Neville, Tim. "Colin O'Brady Wants to Tell You a Story." *Outside Online*, August 15, 2019. *https://www.outsideonline.com/2400795/colin -obrady-profile-antarctica.*

NGSS Hub. Accessed December 6, 2018. *https://ngss.nsta.org/Display Standard.aspx?view=pe&id=225.*

"Northwest Passage | Trade Route, North America." *Encyclopedia Britannica* . Accessed September 11, 2019. *https://www.britannica.com/place /Northwest-Passage-trade-route.*

O'Brady, Colin. *Colin O'Brady (@colinobrady) • Instagram Photos and Videos*. Accessed December 8, 2018. *https://www.instagram.com/colinobrady/.*

—. *Next Level Testing with Standard Process. YouTube*, June 10, 2018. *https:// www.youtube.com/watch?v=JmvNSoNjCcY.*

Out of the Crevasse Field. August 30, 2005. *https://earthobservatory.nasa. gov/features/Crevasse/crevasse2.php.*

Palmer, Richard. "William and Harry Pay Emotional Tribute to Their Friend Who Tried to Cross the Antarctic." *Express.Co.Uk*, January 17, 2017. *https://www.express.co.uk/news/royal/755461/William-Harry -emotional-tribute-friend-died-Antarctic.*

Pattison, Mark. "020: Colin O'Brady, from Being Burned on 25% of His Body to Becoming the Fastest Person to Climb the Seven Summits & Ski to the North and South Pole All in 139 Days. Wow!" *Mark Pattison NFL*, October 20, 2017. *https://www.markpattisonnfl.com/020-colin-obrady -peak-inspiration/.*

Petrovic, Karli. "Colin O'Brady: What Inspired the Elite Mountain Climber to Smash World Records." *Alive*, April 25, 2017. *https://www.alive.com /lifestyle/beating-the-odds-again-and-again/.*

Phillips, Eric. *Eric.Philips.98. Facebook.* Accessed March 14, 2020. *https:// www.facebook.com/eric.phillips.98.*

Polar Mission Army Explorer Appointed MBE. June 8, 2018. *www.bbc.com, https://www.bbc.com/news/uk-wales-mid-wales-44413421.*

Ragogna, Mike. "Ain't No Mountain High Enough: A Conversation with Colin O'Brady." *Huffington Post*, March 8, 2016. *https://www.huffingtonpost .com/entry/aint-no-mountain-high-enough-a-conversation-with _us_56dde9fae4b0a94557aab697.*

"Record-Breaking Mountain Climber's Next Feat? Fighting Childhood Obesity." *TODAY.Com.* Accessed March 9, 2019. *https://www.today.com /health/elite-mountain-climber-colin-o-brady-fights-childhood -obesity-t97706.*

Removal of the Sledge Dogs—British Antarctic Survey. Accessed May 17, 2019. *https://www.bas.ac.uk/about/antarctica/environmental-protection /wildlife-and-plants-2/removal-of-the-sledge-dogs/.*

Rogan, Joe. *Joe Rogan Experience #1244—Colin O'Brady.* 2019. *YouTube, https://www.youtube.com/watch?v=1Gtrg6R7b3w.*

Roll, Rich. "Doing the Impossible with Colin O'Brady." *YouTube*, May 6, 2019. *https://www.youtube.com/channel/UCpjlh0e319ksmo OD7bQFSiw.*

Routen, Ash. "Lou Rudd Announces Plan to Cross Antarctica Alone and Un- supported." Accessed February 15, 2019. *Explorersweb, https://explorer sweb.com/2018/04/23/lou-rudd-announces-plan-to-cross-antarctica -alone-and-unsupported-2018-04-07-10377-2/.*

Rudd, Lou. "Spirit of Endurance." *Louis Rudd MBE*, April 1, 2018. *https://lourudd.com/2018/04/01/the-journey-begins/.*

Rush, Richard. "Explorer Returns to His Holbeach Roots." *The Voice*. Accessed February 17, 2019. *https://www.spaldingvoice.co.uk/explorer-returns-to-his-holbeach-roots/.*

Scott, Robert Falcon. *Scott's Last Journey*. Edited by Peter King, Gerald Duckworth, 1999.

—. *The Voyage of the Discovery*. Scribner, 1907.

Shackell, James. "Zen and Calories: Secrets of the First Man to Walk Solo Across Antarctica." *Adventure.Com*, June 3, 2019. *http://serebral360traveler.com/2019/06/03/zen-and-calories-secrets-of-the-first-man-to-walk-solo-across-antarctica-by-james-shackell-adventure//.*

Skolnick, Adam. "Colin O'Brady Completes Crossing of Antarctica with Final 32-Hour Push." *New York Times*, December 26, 2018. *NYTimes.com*, *https://www.nytimes.com/2018/12/26/sports/antarctica-race-colin-obrady.html.*

—. "Louis Rudd Completes His Trek Across Antarctica 2 Days Behind Colin O'Brady." *New York Times*, December 28, 2018. *https://www.nytimes.com/2018/12/28/sports/louis-rudd-antarctica-colin-obrady.html.*

—. "Reflections on Antarctica." *New York Times*, January 18, 2019. *https://www.nytimes.com/2019/01/18/sports/reflections-on-antarctica.html.*

—. "Tracking the Race Across Antarctica." *New York Times*, December 18, 2018. *https://www.nytimes.com/interactive/2018/12/18/sports/antarctica-race-tracker-map.html.*

Skolnick, Adam, and Tamara Merino. "No One Has Ever Crossed Antarctica Unsupported. Two Men Are Trying Right Now." *New York Times*, March 12, 2019. *https://www.nytimes.com/2018/11/11/sports/antarctica-race.html.*

Smith, Julian. "The Inside Tale of Colin O'Brady's Death-Defying, Record-Breaking Antarctic Crossing." *Portland Monthly*. Accessed November 2, 2019. *https://www.pdxmonthly.com/articles/2019/3/26/the-inside-tale-of-colin-obradys-death-defying-record-breaking-antarctic-crossing.*

Soldier's Solo Antarctica Crossing Bid. October 17, 2018. *www.bbc.com*, *https://www.bbc.com/news/uk-wales-45888276.*

Solomon, Susan. *The Coldest March: Scott's Fatal Antarctic Expedition*. Yale University Press, 2002.

Standard Process—Colin O'Brady. Accessed April 7, 2019. *https://www.standardprocess.com/Campaign/Colin-OBrady#.XKpH9etKhN0.*

Struthers, Dan, and Jack Hudson. "My Mate Lou." *Shackleton London*. Accessed March 4, 2019. *https://shackletonlondon.com/blogs/pre-expedition/my-mate-lou.*

Sunrise and Sunset Times in South Pole, March 2019. Accessed February 28, 2019. *https://www.timeanddate.com/sun/antarctica/south -pole?month=3.*

"Survival Clothing in the Early 1900s." *Shackleton London.* Accessed February 22, 2019. *https://shackletonlondon.com/blogs/blog/equipped-for -survival.*

Synnott, Mark. "Free Solo Across Antarctica." *National Geographic,* November 2, 2018. *https://www.nationalgeographic.com/adventure/2018/11 /antarctica-solo-unaided-cross-ski-attempt-colin-obrady/.*

—. "This Man Is Walking Across Antarctica All By Himself." *National Geographic News,* November 9, 2015. *https://news.nationalgeographic .com/2015/11/151109-south-pole-antarctic-explorers-shackleton -expedition/.*

Teasdale, Aaron. "Antarctic Explorers Enter No-Rescue Zone." *National Geographic.* Accessed August 25, 2019. *https://www.nationalgeographic .com/adventure/2018/12/antarctic-explorers-enter-no-rescue-zone/.*

—. "Explorer Crosses South Pole in Epic Race across Antarctica." *National Geographic,* December 13, 2018. *https://www.nationalgeographic.com /adventure/2018/12/explorers-colin-obrady-louis-rudd-race-south -pole-antarctica/.*

—. "Second Explorer Completes Antarctic Crossing." *National Geographic,* December 28, 2018. *https://www.nationalgeographic.com/adventure /2018/12/second-explorer-louis-rudd-crosses-antarctica/.*

Terra Nova, Scott, South Pole—Ships of the Antarctic Explorers. Accessed December 1, 2018. *https://www.coolantarctica.com/Antarctica%20 fact%20file/History/antarctic_ships/terra_nova.php.*

The Gjøa Expedition (1903–1906)—FramMuseum.No. Accessed March 3, 2019. *http://frammuseum.no/polar_history/expeditions/the_Gjøa _expedition__1903-1906_/.*

The Polar Ship Fram-FramMuseum.No. Accessed December 1, 2018. *http:// frammuseum.no/polar_history/vessels/the_polar_ship_fram/.*

Turley, Charles. *The Voyages of Captain Scott.* Dodd, Mead and Company, 1915.

Walsh, Martin. "Antarctica 2019-2020: Expeditions to Watch." *Explorersweb,* November 11, 2019. *https://explorersweb.com/2019/11/11/antarctica -2019-2020-expeditions-to-watch/.*

Wang, Andrew. "IM 017: Setting Small Goals to Achieve the Extraordinary | Colin O'Brady | Transcript." *Runnymede Capital Management.* Accessed March 10, 2019. *http://www.runnymede.com/017-transcript/.*

Williams, Isobel P. "Shackleton's Scurvy—or Its Absence." *Isobel Williams— Author, Cruise Speaker and Lecturer,* October 5, 2018. *https://isobelp williams.com/2018/10/05/shackletons-scurvy-or-its-absence/.*

Windsor, Peter. "O'Brady's Antarctic Crossing: Was It Really Unassisted?" *Explorersweb*. Accessed May 15, 2019. *https://explorersweb .com/2018/12/27/obradys-antarctic-crossing-was-it-really-unassisted/*.

Woolhouse, Megan. "Exploring Endurance." *BU Today*. Accessed March 20, 2019. *http://www.bu.edu/bostonia/winter-spring19/exploring -endurance/*.

ENDNOTES

1 "I write the history . . . different from what I had imagined." Roald Amundsen, *The South Pole: An Account of the Norwegian Antarctic Expedition in the "Fram," 1910–1912*, p. 12.

2 "So here we are . . . ought to get through." Robert Scott, *Scott's Last Journey*, p. 144.

3 "It is odds that the dog rather than the man directs the walk." Robert Scott, *Voyage of the Discovery Vol. I*, p. 286.

4 "forced to reinstate . . . ask for leave." David Crane, *Scott of the Antarctic: A Life of Courage and Tragedy*, p. 229.

5 "I am . . . routine." David Crane, *Scott of the Antarctic: A Life of Courage and Tragedy*, p. 291.

6 "the key to everything." David Crane, *Scott of the Antarctic: A Life of Courage and Tragedy*, p. 337.

7 "no journey ever made . . . splendidly won." Robert Scott, *Voyage of the Discovery Vol. I*, p. 343.

8 "The main object . . . that achievement." Elspeth Huxley, *Scott of the Antarctic*, p. 181.

9 "Whatever I have accomplished . . . conscientious work." Roald Amundsen, *My Life as an Explorer*, p. 1.

10 "she is not adapted for very heavy seas, and may turn turtle [roll over]." Robert Scott, *Scott's Last Journey*, p. 76.

11 "This was a blow indeed!" Amundsen, *My Life as an Explorer*, p. 64.

12 "If the expedition . . . without hesitation." Amundsen, *The South Pole: An Account of the Norwegian Antarctic Expedition in the "Fram," 1910–1912*, p. 22.

13 "Everything had to be got ready quietly and calmly." Roald Amundsen, *The South Pole: An Account of the Norwegian Antarctic Expedition in the "Fram," 1910–1912*, p. 22.

14 "were the only practicable . . . can traverse." Roald Amundsen, *My Life as an Explorer*, p. 66.

15 "The dog must understand . . . make himself respected." Roald Amundsen, *The South Pole: An Account of the Norwegian Antarctic Expedition in the "Fram," 1910–1912*, p. 25.

16 "upon whose . . . blindly rely." Roald Amundsen, *The South Pole: An Account of the Norwegian Antarctic Expedition in the "Fram," 1910–1912*, p. 22.

17 "As the names . . . 'Yes' ready." Roald Amundsen, *The South Pole: An Account of the Norwegian Antarctic Expedition in the "Fram," 1910–1912*, p. 42.

18 "BEG LEAVE . . . AMUNDSEN." Robert Scott, *Scott's Last Journey*, p. 45.

19 "I know . . . sweeter." Colin O'Brady, *Instagram* (Oct. 16, 2018), *https://www.instagram.com/p/BpAIv4pFJwd/*.

20 "I am . . . task." Louis Rudd, "The Journey Begins," *Spirit of Endurance Blog* (April 1, 2018), *https://lourudd.com/2018/04/01/the-journey-begins/*

21 "Get wet, you die." David Grann, "Retracing the Antarctic Journey of Henry Worsley," *New Yorker* (Oct. 31, 2018), *https://www.newyorker.com/news/news-desk/retracing-the-antarctic-journey-of-henry-worsley*

22 "the sheer vastness of Antarctica." "Lou Rudd to Begin Attempt to Traverse Antarctic Continent—The Spirit of Endurance Expedition," *The Great Outdoors* (Oct. 24, 2018), *https://www.tgomagazine.co.uk/news/lou-rudd-to-begin-attempt-to-traverse-antarctic-continent-the-spirit-of-endurance-expedition/*

23 "I knew absolutely nothing . . . taught me everything." "Lou Rudd to Begin Attempt to Traverse Antarctic Continent—The Spirit of Endurance Expedition," *The Great Outdoors* (Oct. 24, 2018), *https://www.tgomagazine.co.uk/news/lou-rudd-to-begin-attempt-to-traverse-antarctic-continent-the-spirit-of-endurance-expedition/*

24 "More people . . . traversed Antarctica."

Louis Rudd, *Spear 17 Blog, https://lou-rudd.com/spear17/*

25   "they were . . . on skis." Louis Rudd, *Spear 17 Blog, https://lourudd.com/spear17/*

26   "Like a siren song . . . she draws you back." "Lou Rudd to Begin Attempt to Traverse Antarctic Continent—The Spirit of Endurance Expedition," *The Great Outdoors* (Oct. 24, 2018), *https://www.tgomagazine.co.uk/news/lou-rudd-to-begin-attempt-to-traverse-antarctic-continent-the-spirit-of-endurance-expedition/*

27   "It's right at the limits." "Lou Rudd to Begin Attempt to Traverse Antarctic Continent—The Spirit of Endurance Expedition," *The Great Outdoors* (Oct. 24, 2018), *https://www.tgomagazine.co.uk/news/lou-rudd-to-begin-attempt-to-traverse-antarctic-conti-nent-the-spirit-of-endurance-expedi-tion/*

28   "20 kg tire through quite long grass." Paul Kirtley, "PK Podcast 034: Lou Rudd on the Motivation to Traverse Antarctica Solo, Unsupported and Unaided," *Paul Kirtley Podcast* (Nov. 19, 2018), *https://paulkirtley.co.uk/2018/lou-rudd-on-the-motivation-to-tra-verse-antarctica-solo-unsupported-and-unaided/*

29   "Mr. A-minus." Michael Gervais, "Colin O'Brady: Explorers Grand Slam," *Finding Mastery Podcast* (July 20, 2016), *https://findingmastery.net/colin-obrady/*

30   "Don't you . . . your hardest?" Michael Gervais, "Colin O'Brady: Explorers Grand Slam," *Finding Mastery Podcast* (July 20, 2016), *https://findingmas-tery.net/colin-obrady/*

31   "terribly wrong." Joe Rogan, "Joe Rogan Experience #1244—Colin O'Brady," *Joe Rogan Experience* (Feb. 11, 2019), *https://www.youtube.com/watch?v=1Gtrg6R7b3w*

32   "Instinct takes over." Joe Rogan, "Joe Rogan Experience #1244—Colin O'Brady," *Joe Rogan Experience* (Feb. 11, 2019), *https://www.youtube.com/watch?v=1Gtrg6R7b3w*

33   "the darkest time of my life." Joe Rogan, "Joe Rogan Experience #1244—Colin O'Brady," *Joe Rogan Experience* (Feb. 11, 2019),

https://www.youtube.com/watch?v=1Gtrg6R7b3w

34   "It was like . . . away from me." Julian Smith, "The Inside Tale of Colin O'Brady's Death-Defying, Record-Breaking Antarctic Crossing," *Portland Monthly* (March 26, 2019), *https://www.pdxmonthly.com/articles/2019/3/26/the-inside-tale-of-colin-obradys-death-defying-record-breaking-antarctic-crossing*

35   "Let's stay positive." Erin Beresini, "Seeing the World—One Tri or Summit at a Time," *USA Triathlon, https://www.teamusa.org/USA-Triathlon/About/USAT/Magazine/Colin-OBrady-Fall-2016*

36   "Let's set a goal together." Beresini, *Seeing the World—One Tri or Summit at a Time, https://www.teamusa.org/USA-Triathlon/About/USAT/Magazine/Colin-OBrady-Fall-2016*

37   "crossing the finish . . . done be-fore." Joe Rogan, "Joe Rogan Experience #1244—Colin O'Brady," *Joe Rogan Experience* (Feb. 11, 2019), *https://www.youtube.com/watch?v=1Gtrg6R7b3w*

38   "I literally have . . . a triath-lon now!" Joe Rogan, "Joe Rogan Experience #1244—Colin O'Brady," *Joe Rogan Experience* (Feb. 11, 2019), *https://www.youtube.com/watch?v=1Gtrg6R7b3w*

39   "complete and utter surprise." Joe Rogan, "Joe Rogan Experience #1244—Colin O'Brady," *Joe Rogan Experience* (Feb. 11, 2019), *https://www.youtube.com/watch?v=1Gtrg6R7b3w*

40   "You're strong . . . shall pass." Hilary Brueck, "The 33-year-old who just became the first person to cross Antarctica alone says 2 simple mantras were crucial to his success," *Business Insider* (Jan. 15, 2019), *https://www.businessinsider.com/colin-obrady-crossed-antarctica-with-two-simple-mantras-2019-1?r=US&IR=T*

41   "you have . . . lose weight." James Shackell, "Zen and calories: secrets of the first man to walk solo across Antarctica," *Adventure.com* (June 3, 2019), *http://serebral360traveler.com/2019/06/03/zen-and-calories-secrets-of-the-first-man-to-walk-solo-*

across-antarctica-by-james-shackell-adventure/

42　"would do . . . ice buckets." Colin O'Brady, *Instagram* (May 19, 2019), *https://www.instagram.com/p/BxP5ZeXFo_v/*

43　"I came . . . the new project." Colin O'Brady, *Instagram* (Sept. 14, 2018), *https://www.instagram.com/p/BnuVcwwlx_W/*

44　"ANNOUNCING . . . the ice." Colin O'Brady, *Instagram* (Oct. 18, 2018), *https://www.instagram.com/p/BpFh0S9lqtd/*

45　"Strangely enough . . . Arctic explorer." Roald Amundsen, *My Life as an Explorer*, pp. 2–3.

46　"My story . . . can be turned." Scott, *Voyage of the Discovery Vol. I*, p. 24.

47　"I may . . . Polar exploration." Scott, *Voyage of the Discovery Vol. I*, p. 24.

48　"awful." Scott, *Scott's Last Journey*, p. 153.

49　"geographical . . . to the south." Scott, *Voyage of the Discovery Vol. I*, p. 61.

50　"The very vastness . . . mystery." Huxley, *Scott of the Antarctic*, p. 63.

51　"We determined . . . utmost limit." Ranulph Fiennes, *Race to the Pole: Tragedy, Heroism, and Scott's Antarctic Quest*, p. 88.

52　"to the regret of all of us." Scott, *Voyage of the Discovery Vol. I*, p. 53.

53　"insisted on . . . bitterest weather." Roald Amundsen, *My Life as an Explorer*, p. 3.

54　"increasing my skill . . . great adventure." Roald Amundsen, *My Life as an Explorer*, p. 3.

55　"read all . . . hands on." Amundsen, *My Life as an Explorer*, p. 19.

56　"baffling mystery . . . the past." Amundsen, *My Life as an Explorer*, p. 37.

57　"TEIMA!" . . . "manik-ut-mi!" Roald Amundsen, *To the North Magnetic Pole and Through the Northwest Passage*, p. 257.

58　"fur garments . . . this climate." Roald Amundsen, *To the North Magnetic Pole and Through the Northwest Passage*, p. 262.

59　"I could not . . . every pitfall." Amundsen, *My Life as an Explorer*, p. 51.

60　"What a glorious sight . . . the west!" Roald Amundsen, *My Life as an Explorer*, p. 51.

61　"When it's blue sky . . . endless sea of light." Adam Skolnick, "Reflections on Antarctica," *New York Times* (Jan. 18, 2019), *https://www.nytimes.com/2019/01/18/sports/reflections-on-antarctica.html*

62　"It's a place . . . bit of both!" "Lou Rudd to Begin Attempt to Traverse Antarctic Continent—The Spirit of Endurance Expedition," *The Great Outdoors* (Oct. 24, 2018), *https://www.tgomagazine.co.uk/news/lou-rudd-to-begin-attempt-to-traverse-antarctic-continent-the-spirit-of-endurance-expedition/*

63　"absolutely gobsmacked by this epic journey." *Shackleton London, Lou's Antarctic Journey (Part One)* (Jan. 16, 2019), *https://www.youtube.com/watch?v=Bsoybzf2C_E*

64　"That was the first . . . extreme trip." Paul Kirtley, "PK Podcast 012: Lou Rudd on Unsupported Polar Journeys and Retracing Amundsen's Route to the South Pole," *Paul Kirtley Podcast* (Jan. 7, 2016), *http://paulkirtley.co.uk/2016/lou-rudd-unsupported-polar-journeys-retracing-amundsens-route-south-pole/*

65　"We're sharing . . . drag, mate.'" Paul Kirtley, "PK Podcast 012: Lou Rudd on Unsupported Polar Journeys and Retracing Amundsen's Route to the South Pole," *Paul Kirtley Podcast* (Jan. 7, 2016), *http://paulkirtley.co.uk/2016/lou-rudd-unsupported-polar-journeys-retracing-amundsens-route-south-pole/*

66　"It's so vast . . . the planet." Ash Routen, "Lou Rudd Announces Plan to Cross Antarctica Alone and Unsupported," *Explorer's Web* (April 23, 2018), *https://explorersweb.com/2018/04/23/lou-rudd-announces-plan-to-cross-antarctica-alone-and-unsupported-2018-04-07-10377-2/*

67　"grazing bag . . . constantly coming in." Paul Kirtley, "PK Podcast 012: Lou Rudd on Unsupported Polar Journeys and Retracing Amundsen's Route to the

South Pole," *Paul Kirtley Podcast* (Jan. 7, 2016), *http://paulkirtley.co.uk/2016/lou-rudd-unsupported-polar-journeys-retracing-amundsens-route-south-pole/*

68 "As a husband . . . this trip." Louis Rudd, "Post Expedition Reflection" (Jan. 14, 2019), *https://lourudd.com/2019/01/14/post-expedition-reflection/*

69 "As a fitting tribute . . . his journey." Louis Rudd, "The Journey Begins," *Spirit of Endurance* (April 1, 2018), *https://lourudd.com/2018/04/01/the-journey-begins/*

70 "Because your body's . . . absolute cleanest." Rich Roll, "Doing the Impossible with Colin O'Brady," *Rich Roll Podcast* (May 6, 2019), *https://www.youtube.com/watch?v=10xhj49PUvo*

71 "They're quite good." Rich Roll, "Doing the Impossible with Colin O'Brady," *Rich Roll Podcast* (May 6, 2019), *https://www.youtube.com/watch?v=10xhj49PUvo*

72 "This journey . . . inside all of us." Colin O'Brady, *Instagram* (Oct. 18, 2018), *https://www.instagram.com/p/BpFh0S9lqtd/*

73 "Every day . . . some crevasse." Roald Amundsen, *The South Pole: An Account of the Norwegian Antarctic Expedition in the "Fram," 1910–1912*, p. 144.

74 "There is rather . . . more troublesome . . ." Robert Scott, *Scott's Last Journey*, p. 132.

75 "We are captured." Robert Scott, *Scott's Last Journey*, p. 33.

76 "a sheer waste of coal." Robert Scott, *Scott's Last Journey*, p. 29.

77 "I can imagine . . . worst of conditions." Robert Scott, *Scott's Last Journey*, p. 37.

78 "behaved splendidly . . . through so well." Scott, *Scott's Last Journey*, p. 37.

79 "The hut . . . dwelling-place imaginable." Robert Scott, *Scott's Last Journey*, p. 61.

80 "The peace . . . these days." Robert Scott, *Scott's Last Journey*, p. 40.

81 "was perfectly excellent . . . the animals." Robert Scott, *Scott's Last Journey*, p. 63.

82 "splendid work . . . a ship." Robert Scott, *Scott's Last Expedition*, p. 100.

83 "just a cairn . . . a bamboo [stick]." Apsley Cherry-Garrard, *The Worst Journey in the World*, p. 113.

84 "sometimes a blizzard is a welcome rest." Apsley Cherry-Garrard, *The Worst Journey in the World*, p. 110.

85 "every incident pales before." Robert Scott, *Scott's Last Journey*, p. 75.

86 "extremely kind." Roald Amundsen, *The South Pole: An Account of the Norwegian Antarctic Expedition in the "Fram," 1910–1912*, p. 69.

87 "The mystic Barrier . . . apprehensive awe." Roald Amundsen, *The South Pole: An Account of the Norwegian Antarctic Expedition in the "Fram," 1910–1912*, p. 57.

88 "so that the ascent . . . gentle slope." Roald Amundsen, *The South Pole: An Account of the Norwegian Antarctic Expedition in the "Fram," 1910–1912*, p. 57.

89 "The dogs . . . else to do." Roald Amundsen, *The South Pole: An Account of the Norwegian Antarctic Expedition in the "Fram," 1910–1912*, p. 60.

90 "One can never . . . looks the same." Roald Amundsen, *The South Pole: An Account of the Norwegian Antarctic Expedition in the "Fram," 1910–1912*, p. 72.

91 "our eyes . . . pegs were found." Roald Amundsen, *The South Pole: An Account of the Norwegian Antarctic Expedition in the "Fram," 1910–1912*, p. 73.

92 "which stood out . . . easy to see." Roald Amundsen, *The South Pole: An Account of the Norwegian Antarctic Expedition in the "Fram," 1910–1912*, p. 75.

93 "Our fight . . . south as possible." Roald Amundsen, *The South Pole: An Account of the Norwegian Antarctic Expedition in the "Fram," 1910–1912*, p. 76.

94 "frankly confessed . . . so well." Roald Amundsen, *The South Pole: An Account of the Norwegian Antarctic Expedition in the "Fram," 1910–1912*, p. 82.

95 "As much as . . . my mental strength." Colin O'Brady, *Instagram* (Oct. 20, 2018), *https://www.instagram.com/p/BpKST8CFwYH/*

96   "Staying focused . . . aspiring adventurers." Louis Rudd, "Steady Progress,"
Louis Rudd MBE (July 17, 2018),
*https://lourudd.com/2018/07/17/
steady-progress/*

97   "whenever he's finished . . . on my
phone," Jack Hudson, "Watchkeeper
(Wendy Searle Interview)" (Nov. 20,
2018) *Shackleton London, https://
shackletonlondon.com/blogs/
pre-expedition/watchkeeper*

98   "needed a comprehensive list . . . you
have that?" Stephen Jones, personal
interview (April 2, 2018).

99   "reserve the right . . . the evening
before." Stephen Jones, personal interview (April 2, 2018).

100   "brilliance . . . just a dream." Colin
O'Brady, *Instagram* (Oct. 30, 2018),
*https://www.instagram.com/p/
BplVCIZF3bU/*

101   "there are . . . Frozen Continent."
Colin O'Brady, *Instagram* (Oct. 26,
2018), *https://www.instagram.com/
colinobrady/p/BpZ8_4AlWE3/?hl=ro*

102   "it will . . . on the ice." Colin O'Brady,
Instagram (Oct. 26, 2018), *https://
www.instagram.com/colinobrady/p/
BpZ8_4AlWE3/?hl=ro*

103   "skiway." Stephen Jones, personal
interview (April 2, 2018).

104   "There's nothing . . . departure."
Stephen Jones, personal interview
(April 2, 2018).

105   "it starts a clock ticking." Stephen Jones,
personal interview (April 2, 2018).

106   "Everything they send . . . told us."
Stephen Jones, personal interview
(April 2, 2018).

107   "'We've been lucky . . . very far down.'"
Roald Amundsen, *The South Pole: An
Account of the Norwegian Antarctic
Expedition in the "Fram," 1910–1912*,
p. 125.

108   "I write this . . . will give way." Robert
Scott, *Scott's Last Expedition*, p. 144.

109   "At best . . . worst in the world." Roald
Amundsen, *My Life as an Explorer*, p. 67.

110   "I tried . . . painted black." Roald
Amundsen, *The South Pole: An Account
of the Norwegian Antarctic Expedition
in the "Fram," 1910–1912*, p. 115.

111   "it was light . . . much appreciated."

Roald Amundsen, *The South Pole: An
Account of the Norwegian Antarctic
Expedition in the "Fram," 1910–1912*,
p. 121.

112   "Our coursers . . . we were off." Roald
Amundsen, *The South Pole: An Account
of the Norwegian Antarctic Expedition
in the "Fram," 1910–1912*, p. 123.

113   "We expected them . . . ski to the Pole!"
Roald Amundsen, *The South Pole: An
Account of the Norwegian Antarctic
Expedition in the "Fram," 1910–1912*,
p. 128.

114   "Scott's route was out of bounds."
Roald Amundsen, *The South Pole: An
Account of the Norwegian Antarctic
Expedition in the "Fram," 1910–1912*,
p. 24.

115   "what struck . . . covered with snow."
Roald Amundsen, *The South Pole: An
Account of the Norwegian Antarctic
Expedition in the "Fram," 1910–1912*,
p. 131.

116   If this . . . smashing it." Roald
Amundsen, *The South Pole: An Account
of the Norwegian Antarctic Expedition
in the "Fram," 1910–1912*, p. 134.

117   "was unusually industrious in stirring it." Roald Amundsen, *The South
Pole: An Account of the Norwegian
Antarctic Expedition in the "Fram,"
1910–1912*, p. 138.

118   "Twenty-four . . . of our dogs." Roald
Amundsen, *The South Pole: An Account
of the Norwegian Antarctic Expedition
in the "Fram," 1910–1912*, p. 138.

119   "Bowers is . . . quite unselfish." Robert
Scott, *Scott's Last Journey*, pp. 118–119.

120   "I don't like . . . is pleasant." Robert
Scott, *Scott's Last Journey*, p. 125.

121   "We could see . . . in the face." Robert
Scott, *Scott's Last Journey*, p. 133.

122   "We men are . . . much depends."
Robert Scott, *Scott's Last Journey*,
p. 127.

123   "began to cross . . . some mile apart."
Apsley Cherry-Garrard, *The Worst
Journey in the World*, p. 335.

124   "a great white line of jagged edges, the
chaos of pressure." Apsley Cherry-
Garrard, *The Worst Journey in the
World*, p. 337.

125   "Our case . . . to his belly in it . . ."

Robert Scott, *Scott's Last Journey*, p. 136.

126 "the temperature remains +33°, and everything is disgustingly wet." Robert Scott, *Scott's Last Journey*, p. 136.

127 "Thank God . . . we begin the heavier work ourselves." Robert Scott, *Scott's Last Journey*, p. 137 note.

128 "the snow . . . the sledges," Robert Scott, *Scott's Last Journey*, p. 139.

129 "there does not . . . men and true." Robert Scott, *Scott's Last Journey*, p. 111 note.

130 "dreaded . . . heartrending." Robert Scott, *Scott's Last Journey*, p. 144.

131 "We are . . . against odds," Robert Scott, *Scott's Last Journey*, p. 144.

132 "Full of emotion . . . quite so apropos." Colin O'Brady, *Instagram* (Nov. 3, 2018), *https://www.instagram.com/p/ BpvVqEEFwef/*

133 "To be finally . . . really eerie." Louis Rudd, "The First Day (Log #2)," *Shackleton London* (Nov. 3, 2018), *https://shackletonlon-don.com/blogs/lou-s-journal/ lous-expedition-update-2*

134 "Don't tell me . . . I ask." Davey Braun, "Alone Across Antarctica Part 2: Captain Louis Rudd—For the Love of the Journey," *The Outdoor Journal* (July 15, 2019), *https://www.outdoor-journal.com/featured/athletes-and-explorers/captain-louis-rudd-antarc-tica-crossing/*

135 "Really tough going." Louis Rudd, "The First Day (Log #2)," *Shackleton London* (Nov. 3, 2018), *https://shackle-tonlondon.com/blogs/lou-s-journal/ lous-expedition-update-2*

136 "The only way . . . by skiing," Paul Kirtley, "PK Podcast 034: Lou Rudd on the Motivation to Traverse Antarctica Solo, Unsupported and Unaided," *Paul Kirtley Podcast* (Nov. 18, 2018), *https:// paulkirtley.co.uk/2018/lou-rudd-on-the-motivation-to-traverse-antarcti-ca-solo-unsupported-and-unaided/*

137 "3:00 am . . . cold-weather camping." Davey Braun, "Alone Across Antarctica Part 2: Captain Louis Rudd—For the Love of the Journey," *The Outdoor Journal* (July 15, 2019), *https://www. outdoorjournal.com/featured/*

athletes-and-explorers/captain-louis-rudd-antactica-crossing/

138 "a bit of a speck in the distance." Louis Rudd, "Tough Battle (Log #3)," *Shackleton London* (Nov. 4, 2018), *https://shackletonlon-don.com/blogs/lou-s-journal/ lous-expedition-update-3*

139 "things can only get better as the pulk gets lighter." Louis Rudd, "Tough Battle (Log #3)," *Shackleton London* (Nov. 4, 2018), *https://shackleton-london.com/blogs/lou-s-journal/ lous-expedition-update-3*

140 "jerk forward . . . all day . . ." Louis Rudd, "Tough Battle (Log #3)," *Shackleton London* (Nov. 4, 2018), *https://shackletonlon-don.com/blogs/lou-s-journal/ lous-expedition-update-3*

141 "flat on my back . . . nowhere." Louis Rudd, "Music on Ice (Log #6)," *Shackleton London* (Nov. 8, 2018), *https://shackletonlondon.com/blogs/ lou-s-journal/lous-expedition-log-6*

142 "Maybe we didn't get it right." Rich Roll, "Doing the Impossible with Colin O'Brady," *Rich Roll Podcast* (May 6, 2019), *https://www.youtube.com/ watch?v=10xhj49PUvo*

143 "Just get . . . feel better." Rich Roll, "Doing the Impossible with Colin O'Brady," *Rich Roll Podcast* (May 6, 2019), *https://www.youtube.com/ watch?v=10xhj49PUvo*

144 "to walk . . . shock absorber." Julian Smith, "The Inside Tale of Colin O'Brady's Death-Defying, Record-Breaking Antarctic Crossing," *Portland Monthly* (March 26, 2019), *https://www.pdxmonthly.com/ articles/2019/3/26/the-inside-tale-of-colin-obradys-death-defying-record-breaking-antarctic-crossing*

145 "perhaps a little . . . at hand." Colin O'Brady, *Instagram* (Nov. 3, 2018), *https://www.instagram.com/p/ BpvVqEEFwef/*

146 "Tomorrow . . . inner peace." Rich Roll, "Doing the Impossible with Colin O'Brady," *Rich Roll Podcast* (May 6, 2019), *https://www.youtube.com/ watch?v=10xhj49PUvo*

147 "We are . . . capable." Rich Roll, "Doing the Impossible with Colin

O'Brady," *Rich Roll Podcast* (May 6, 2019), *https://www.youtube.com/watch?v=10xhj49PUvo*

148 "calm my mind." Rich Roll, "Doing the Impossible with Colin O'Brady," *Rich Roll Podcast* (May 6, 2019), *https://www.youtube.com/watch?v=10xhj49PUvo*

149 "like an airplane . . . are your hands?" Rich Roll, "Doing the Impossible with Colin O'Brady," *Rich Roll Podcast* (May 6, 2019), *https://www.youtube.com/watch?v=10xhj49PUvo*

150 "Hey, good morning, mate!" Rich Roll, "Doing the Impossible with Colin O'Brady," *Rich Roll Podcast* (May 6, 2019), *https://www.youtube.com/watch?v=10xhj49PUvo*

151 "Lou, let this be the last time we speak to one another." Rich Roll, "Doing the Impossible with Colin O'Brady," *Rich Roll Podcast* (May 6, 2019), *https://www.youtube.com/watch?v=10xhj49PUvo*

152 "inside a Ping-Pong ball." Adam Skolnick, "Racing Across Antarctica, One Freezing Day at a Time," *New York Times* (Nov. 29, 2018), *https://www.nytimes.com/2018/11/29/sports/antarctica-ski-race.html*

153 "viscerally connected . . . vivid detail." Colin O'Brady, *Instagram* (Nov. 7, 2018), *https://www.instagram.com/p/Bp5nMwblfk2/*

154 "When the weather . . . in every direction." Colin O'Brady, *Instagram* (Nov. 9, 2018), *https://www.instagram.com/p/Bp-0_PLF7ew/*

155 "head down . . . trudge away." Louis Rudd, "Remembrance Day (Log #9)," *Shackleton London* (Nov. 11, 2018), *https://shackletonlondon.com/blogs/lou-s-journal/log-9-remembrance-day*

156 "that's again . . . absolute tonne," Louis Rudd, "Remembrance Day (Log #9)," *Shackleton London* (Nov. 11, 2018), *https://shackletonlondon.com/blogs/lou-s-journal/log-9-remembrance-day*

157 "It looked . . . small scale either." Roald Amundsen, *The South Pole: An Account of the Norwegian Antarctic Expedition in the "Fram," 1910–1912*, p. 143

158 "I never had . . . to ourselves." Roland Huntford, *Race to the South Pole: The Expedition Diaries of Scott and Amundsen*, p. 248.

159 "Amid joking . . . into the blizzard," Roald Amundsen, *The South Pole: An Account of the Norwegian Antarctic Expedition in the "Fram," 1910–1912*, p. 140.

160 "pale blue . . . deepest black." Roald Amundsen, *The South Pole: An Account of the Norwegian Antarctic Expedition in the "Fram," 1910–1912*, pp. 145–146.

161 "Chasm after chasm . . . fearful abyss on each side." Roald Amundsen, *The South Pole: An Account of the Norwegian Antarctic Expedition in the "Fram," 1910–1912*, pp. 145–146.

162 "when I wanted . . . out of breath." Roald Amundsen, *The South Pole: An Account of the Norwegian Antarctic Expedition in the "Fram," 1910–1912*, p. 138.

163 "whether my pulling . . . positively dazzled us." Roald Amundsen, *The South Pole: An Account of the Norwegian Antarctic Expedition in the "Fram," 1910–1912*, p. 150.

164 "jubilant shout." Roald Amundsen, *The South Pole: An Account of the Norwegian Antarctic Expedition in the "Fram," 1910–1912*, p. 150.

165 "All the sledges . . . affected me like this." Roald Amundsen, *The South Pole: An Account of the Norwegian Antarctic Expedition in the "Fram," 1910–1912*, p. 151.

166 "It was . . . at hand." Roald Amundsen, *The South Pole: An Account of the Norwegian Antarctic Expedition in the "Fram," 1910–1912*, p. 153.

167 "not much . . . all the more." Roald Amundsen, *The South Pole: An Account of the Norwegian Antarctic Expedition in the "Fram," 1910–1912*, p. 153.

168 "a vast plain . . . mile after mile." Roald Amundsen, *The South Pole: An Account of the Norwegian Antarctic Expedition in the "Fram," 1910–1912*, p. vii.

169 "Halt!" Roald Amundsen, *The South Pole: An Account of the Norwegian Antarctic Expedition in the "Fram," 1910–1912*, p. 153.

170 "best friends." Roald Amundsen, *The South Pole: An Account of the*

Norwegian Antarctic Expedition in the "Fram," 1910–1912, p. 154.

171 "South Pole, December 14, 1911." Roald Amundsen, *The South Pole: An Account of the Norwegian Antarctic Expedition in the "Fram," 1910–1912*, p. 154.

172 "Good luck . . . to 90°." Roald Amundsen, *The South Pole: An Account of the Norwegian Antarctic Expedition in the "Fram," 1910–1912*, p. 156.

173 the job . . . I expected." Robert Scott, *Scott's Last Journey*, p. 147.

174 "poor old Crean wept." Robert Scott, *Scott's Last Journey*, p. 148.

175 "I am one . . . to be true." Crane, *Scott of the Antarctic: A Life of Courage and Tragedy*, 483.

176 "RECORD." Robert Scott, *Scott's Last Journey*, p. 150 note.

177 "I found . . . still awfully heavy." Robert Scott, *Scott's Last Journey*, p. 150 note.

178 "Oates seems . . . rest of us . . ." Robert Scott, *Scott's Last Journey*, p. 152.

179 "The march is growing terribly monotonous," Robert Scott, *Scott's Last Journey*, p. 150 note.

180 "Our chance . . . trying time." Robert Scott, *Scott's Last Journey*, p. 152.

181 "continued in his indefatigable efforts." Robert Scott, *Scott's Last Journey*, p. 152.

182 "appalling possibility . . . do it now." Robert Scott, *Scott's Last Journey*, p. 152.

183 "near by . . . many dogs." Robert Scott, *Scott's Last Journey*, pp. 152–153.

184 "Great God! . . . reward of priority." Robert Scott, *Scott's Last Journey*, p. 153.

185 "Now for . . . do it." Roland Huntford, *Race to the South Pole: The Expedition Diaries of Scott and Amundsen*, p. 248.

186 "Oates gets cold feet," Robert Scott, *Scott's Last Journey*, p. 161.

187 "a long way . . . tremendous labour." Robert Scott, *Scott's Last Journey*, p. 162.

188 "He is very . . . good sign." Robert Scott, *Scott's Last Journey*, pp. 163–164.

189 "I woke up . . . food and time." Colin O'Brady, *Instagram* (Nov. 29, 2018), *https://www.instagram.com/p/BqyMJxXlHyV/*

190 "Again another really challenging . . . obstacle course, blindfolded." Louis Rudd, "Blindfolded (Log #12)," *Shackleton London* (Nov. 15, 2018), *https://shackletonlondon.com/blogs/lou-s-journal/whiteout-log-12*

191 "You are strong. You are capable." Rich Roll, "Doing the Impossible with Colin O'Brady," *Rich Roll Podcast* (May 6, 2019), *https://www.youtube.com/watch?v=10xhj49PUvo*

192 "loose and deep snow . . . dancing and smiling." Colin O'Brady, *Instagram* (Nov. 19, 2018), *https://www.instagram.com/p/BqYf-_UFDK_/*

193 "I had it . . . lead on him." Adam Skolnick, "Reflections on Antarctica," *New York Times* (Jan. 18, 2019), *https://www.nytimes.com/2019/01/18/sports/reflections-on-antarctica.html*

194 "thick and gloomy." Louis Rudd, "Theils Corner (Log #17)," *Shackleton London* (Nov. 21, 2018), *https://shackletonlondon.com/blogs/lou-s-journal/thiels-corner-log-17*

195 "super-grim. . . . daily routine." Louis Rudd, "A Good Day (Log #25)," *Shackleton London* (Nov. 29, 2018), *https://shackletonlondon.com/blogs/lou-s-journal/a-good-day-log-25*

196 "pretty much snowed . . . this morning." Louis Rudd, "Trust in the GPS (Log #19)," *Shackleton London* (Nov. 23, 2018), *https://shackletonlondon.com/blogs/lou-s-journal/log-19*

197 "It was easy . . . felt fantastic." Adam Skolnick, "Reflections on Antarctica," *New York Times* (Jan. 18, 2019), *https://www.nytimes.com/2019/01/18/sports/reflections-on-antarctica.html*

198 "I can't believe I can't see my tracks." Adam Skolnick, "Reflections on Antarctica," *New York Times* (Jan. 18, 2019), *https://www.nytimes.com/2019/01/18/sports/reflections-on-antarctica.html*

199 "a survival situation." Adam Skolnick, "Reflections on Antarctica," *New York Times* (Jan. 18, 2019), *https://www.nytimes.com/2019/01/18/sports/reflections-on-antarctica.html*

200 "This is getting . . . these conditions."

Adam Skolnick, "Reflections on Antarctica," *New York Times*, (Jan. 18, 2019) *https://www.nytimes.com/2019/01/18/sports/reflections-on-antarctica.html*

201 "stopped dead in [his] tracks." Colin O'Brady, *Instagram*, (Nov. 29, 2018) *https://www.instagram.com/p/BqyMJxXlHyV/*

202 "the most challenging and frustrating day." Colin O'Brady, *Instagram*, (Nov. 29, 2018) *https://www.instagram.com/p/BqyMJxXlHyV/*

203 "pure white. . . . as I was by it." Louis Rudd, "The Bird (Log #29)," *Shackleton London*, (Dec. 3, 2018) *https://shackletonlondon.com/blogs/lou-s-journal/a-feathered-friend-log-29*

204 "I'm not a . . . who It was." Louis Rudd, "The Bird (Log #29)," *Shackleton London*, (Dec. 3, 2018) *https://shackletonlondon.com/blogs/lou-s-journal/a-feathered-friend-log-29*

205 "It's like two tortoises racing each other." Rich Roll, "Doing the Impossible with Colin O'Brady," *Rich Roll Podcast*, (May 6, 2019) *https://www.youtube.com/watch?v=10xhj49PUvo*

206 "we possess . . . very strongly." Colin O'Brady, "10 Days of Silence," *Colin O'Brady*, (Feb. 22, 2017) *https://www.colinobrady.com/blog/2018/2/20/blog-post-template-ef7ct*

207 "committing all of the senses of that moment to memory." Colin O'Brady, *Instagram*, (Dec. 5, 2018) *https://www.instagram.com/p/BrBymR2FUhM/*

208 "Hello . . . stunned." Rich Roll, "Doing the Impossible with Colin O'Brady," *Rich Roll Podcast*, (May 6, 2019) *https://www.youtube.com/watch?v=10xhj49PUvo*

209 "canvas [as] endurance sport." Colin O'Brady, *Instagram*, (Dec. 7, 2018) *https://www.instagram.com/p/BrG8KSnlJlX/*

210 "it was this . . . down my face." Rich Roll, "Doing the Impossible with Colin O'Brady," *Rich Roll Podcast*, (May 6, 2019) *https://www.youtube.com/watch?v=10xhj49PUvo*

211 "I expected to . . . my entire life." Colin O'Brady, *Instagram*, (Dec. 12, 2018) *https://www.instagram.com/p/BrT38WsnSi7/*

212 "all of the love . . . back at you." Colin O'Brady, *Instagram* (Dec. 12, 2018), *https://www.instagram.com/p/BrT38WsnSi7/*

213 "really exciting—sort of like Christmas." Louis Rudd, "The Trudge (Log #39), *Shackleton London* (Dec. 13, 2018), *https://shackletonlondon.com/blogs/lou-s-journal/the-trudge-log-38*

214 "Absolutely epic day . . . quite a celebrity." Louis Rudd, "The South Pole (Log #40)," *Shackleton London* (Dec. 14, 2018), *https://shackleton-london.com/blogs/lou-s-journal/the-south-pole-log-40*

215 "I'm looking down . . . on my arm." Larry Getlen, "How Colin O'Brady Crossed the World's Most Unforgiving Place in 54 Days," *New York Post* (Feb. 22, 2020), *https://www.nytimes.com/interactive/2018/12/18/sports/antarctica-race-tracker-map.html*

216 "Before we began . . . serviceable costume." Roald Amundsen, *The South Pole: An Account of the Norwegian Antarctic Expedition in the "Fram,"* 1910–1912, p. 161.

217 "I wonder . . . the season." Robert Scott, *Scott's Last Journey*, p. 169.

218 "With incredible luck . . . dangerous places." Roald Amundsen, *The South Pole: An Account of the Norwegian Antarctic Expedition in the "Fram,"* 1910–1912, p. 160.

219 "stood there expressing our annoyance rather forcibly." Roald Amundsen, *The South Pole: An Account of the Norwegian Antarctic Expedition in the "Fram,"* 1910–1912, p. 160.

220 "the weather . . . clearest weather." Roald Amundsen, *The South Pole: An Account of the Norwegian Antarctic Expedition in the "Fram,"* 1910–1912, p. 159.

221 "I would readily . . . in my life." Roald Amundsen, *The South Pole: An Account of the Norwegian Antarctic Expedition in the "Fram,"* 1910–1912, p. 161.

222 "it was not . . . the Barrier again." Roald Amundsen, *The South Pole: An Account of the Norwegian Antarctic Expedition in the "Fram,"* 1910–1912, p. 162.

223 "Hullo! . . . by the depot." Roald Amundsen, *The South Pole: An Account*

of the Norwegian Antarctic Expedition in the "Fram," 1910–1912, p. 161.

224 "rather surprised," Roald Amundsen, *The South Pole: An Account of the Norwegian Antarctic Expedition in the "Fram," 1910–1912*, p. 162.

225 "the pace became . . . the sledges." Roald Amundsen, *The South Pole: An Account of the Norwegian Antarctic Expedition in the "Fram," 1910–1912*, p. 162.

226 "I could notice . . . easily and pleasantly." Roald Amundsen, *The South Pole: An Account of the Norwegian Antarctic Expedition in the "Fram," 1910–1912*, p. 162.

227 "to our unspeakable astonishment . . . dear to us." Roald Amundsen, *The South Pole: An Account of the Norwegian Antarctic Expedition in the "Fram," 1910–1912*, p. 164.

228 "What about the Pole? . . . better at home." Roald Amundsen, *The South Pole: An Account of the Norwegian Antarctic Expedition in the "Fram," 1910–1912*, p. 167.

229 "another sick person added to our tent." Roland Huntford, *Race to the South Pole: The Expedition Diaries of Scott and Amundsen*, p. 269.

230 "forty-eight days . . . weather uncertain." Roland Huntford, *Race to the South Pole: The Expedition Diaries of Scott and Amundsen*, p. 272.

231 "wretched day." Roland Huntford, *Race to the South Pole: The Expedition Diaries of Scott and Amundsen*, p. 272.

232 "it is like going ashore . . . so interesting." Roland Huntford, *Race to the South Pole: The Expedition Diaries of Scott and Amundsen*, p. 273.

233 "if this weather . . . reduce food." Robert Scott, *Scott's Last Journey*, p. 166.

234 "the worst ice . . . difficult to cross." Robert Scott, *Scott's Last Journey*, p. 166.

235 "we cannot . . . critical situation." Robert Scott, *Scott's Last Journey*, p. 167.

236 "Evans is . . . being played out." Robert Scott, *Scott's Last Journey*, p. 164.

237 "Evans . . . is going steadily downhill."

Robert Scott, *Scott's Last Journey*, p. 165.

238 "Evans . . . is giving us serious anxiety." Roland Huntford, *Race to the South Pole: The Expedition Diaries of Scott and Amundsen*, p. 278.

239 "Evans has no power to assist with camping work." Robert Scott, *Scott's Last Journey*, p. 167 note.

240 "on his knees . . . complete collapse." Robert Scott, *Scott's Last Journey*, p. 168.

241 "it is a terrible thing . . . so far from home." Robert Scott, *Scott's Last Journey*, p. 168.

242 "continue a . . . marches up." Roland Huntford, *Race to the South Pole: The Expedition Diaries of Scott and Amundsen*, p. 280.

243 "Things must . . . the [next] depot." David Crane, *Scott of the Antarctic: A Life of Courage and Tragedy*, 499.

244 "most rigid economy . . . the next depot." Roland Huntford, *Race to the South Pole: The Expedition Diaries of Scott and Amundsen*, p. 287.

245 "covered with sandy frostrime." Roland Huntford, *Race to the South Pole: The Expedition Diaries of Scott and Amundsen*, p. 288.

246 "God help us. . . . can only guess." Robert Scott, *Scott's Last Journey*, p. 169 note.

247 "misfortunes rarely . . . very bad indeed." Robert Scott, *Scott's Last Journey*, p. 169.

248 "is wonderfully plucky . . . silent in the tent." Robert Scott, *Scott's Last Journey*, p. 170 note.

249 "One feels that for poor Oates the crisis is near." Robert Scott, *Scott's Last Journey*, p. 171.

250 "I doubt whether . . . allowance all round." Robert Scott, *Scott's Last Journey*, p. 171.

251 "Titus Oates . . . the end." Robert Scott, *Scott's Last Journey*, p. 171.

252 "I'm just going outside and may be some time." Robert Scott, *Scott's Last Journey*, p. 173.

253 "It seems a pity . . . our people." Robert Scott, *Scott's Last Journey*, p. 176.

254 "But the hairy . . . arms at this point." Colin O'Brady, *Instagram* (Dec. 16, 2018), *https://www.instagram.com/p/ BreFs1clU_r/*

255 "And my God, . . . over 10kgs already." Louis Rudd, "North (Log #42)," *Shackleton London* (Dec. 16, 2018), *https://shackletonlondon.com/blogs/ lou-s-journal/north*

256 "Every calorie is precious." Colin O'Brady, *Instagram* (Dec. 16, 2018), *https://www.instagram.com/p/ BreFs1clU_r/*

257 "the voice in . . . ripping me apart." Colin O'Brady, *Instagram* (Dec. 19, 2018), *https://www.instagram.com/p/ Brl06yYF54E/*

258 "calmed the storm . . . personal demons." Colin O'Brady, *Instagram* (Dec. 19, 2018), *https://www.instagram. com/p/Brl06yYF54E/*

259 "blowing consistently 35 mph, with gusts over 55 mph." Colin O'Brady, *Instagram* (Dec. 20, 2018), *https://www.instagram.com/p/ BroSy60lyWe/*

260 "broken leg, broken ski, in a sastrugi storm." Rich Roll, "Doing the Impossible with Colin O'Brady," *Rich Roll Podcast* (May 6, 2019), *https://www.youtube.com/ watch?v=10xhj49PUvo*

261 "impossibly hard to reattach in the storm." Rich Roll, "Doing the Impossible with Colin O'Brady," *Rich Roll Podcast* (May 6, 2019), *https://www.youtube.com/ watch?v=10xhj49PUvo*

262 "This too shall pass." Colin O'Brady, *Instagram* (Dec. 19, 2018), *https://www.instagram.com/p/ Brl06yYF54E/*

263 "On your quest . . . be at peace." Rich Roll, "Doing the Impossible with Colin O'Brady," *Rich Roll Podcast* (May 6, 2019), *https://www.youtube.com/ watch?v=10xhj49PUvo*

264 "stuck in an . . . never ending staircase." Colin O'Brady, *Instagram* (Dec. 24, 2018), *https://www.instagram. com/p/BryyJbUldwu/*

265 "People run 100 miles all the time," Adam Skolnick, "Colin O'Brady Completes Crossing of Antarctica with Final 32-Hour Push," *New York Times*, (Dec. 26, 2018), *https://www.nytimes. com/2018/12/26/sports/antarctica- race-colin-obrady.html*

266 "I just locked . . . in complete silence." Rich Roll, "Doing the Impossible with Colin O'Brady," *Rich Roll Podcast* (May 6, 2019), *https://www.youtube.com/ watch?v=10xhj49PUvo*

267 "We had an open . . . he totally delivered." Adam Skolnick, "Colin O'Brady Completes Crossing of Antarctica with Final 32-Hour Push," *New York Times* (Dec. 26, 2018), *https://www.nytimes. com/2018/12/26/sports/antarctica- race-colin-obrady.html*

268 "I was aware . . . live the experience." Adam Skolnick, "Colin O'Brady Completes Crossing of Antarctica With Final 32-Hour Push," *New York Times* (Dec. 26, 2018), *https://www.nytimes. com/2018/12/26/sports/antarctica- race-colin-obrady.html*

269 "I did it! . . . not working?" Rose Minutaglio, "Inside Colin O'Brady's History-Making Solo Trek Across Antarctica," *Esquire* (Jan. 24, 2019), *https://www.esquire.com/news- politics/a25922112/colin-obrady- antarctica-solo-trek-inside/*

270 "Oh, you're bleeding . . . been skiing along!" Louis Rudd, "North (Log #42)," *Shackleton London* (Dec. 16, 2018), *https://shackletonlondon.com/blogs/ lou-s-journal/north*

271 "I noticed that . . . trigger the pain." Louis Rudd, "Beware the Fruit Pastille (Log #45)," *Shackleton London* (Dec. 19, 2018), *https://shackleton- london.com/blogs/lou-s-journal/ beware-the-fruit-pastille-log-45*

272 "throbbed . . . for an hour." Louis Rudd, "Beware the Fruit Pastille (Log #45)," *Shackleton London* (Dec. 19, 2018), *https://shackletonlon- don.com/blogs/lou-s-journal/ beware-the-fruit-pastille-log-45*

273 "a mass of pus and blood." Louis Rudd, "20-Day Plan (Log #41)," *Shackleton London* (Dec. 15, 2018), *https://shack- letonlondon.com/blogs/ lou-s-journal/20-day-plan-log-41*

274 "So the fruit pastilles are gone!" Louis Rudd, "Beware the Fruit Pastille (Log #45)," *Shackleton London* (Dec. 19, 2018), *https://shackletonlondon.com/*

blogs/lou-s-journal/beware-the-fruit -pastille-log-45

275   "All through the night . . . going ten to the dozen." Louis Rudd, "Into the Whiteout (Log #46)," *Shackleton London* (Dec. 20, 2018), *https://shackletonlondon.com/blogs/lou-s-journal/ into-the-whiteout-log-46*

276   "I knew the . . . to go for it." Louis Rudd, "Into the Whiteout (Log #46)," *Shackleton London* (Dec. 20, 2018), *https://shackletonlondon.com/blogs/lou-s-journal/ into-the-whiteout-log-46*

277   "it was still . . . put the tent up." Louis Rudd, "Into the Whiteout (Log #46)," *Shackleton London* (Dec. 20, 2018), *https://shackletonlondon.com/blogs/lou-s-journal/ into-the-whiteout-log-46*

278   "If you rip . . . these conditions." Louis Rudd, "Into the Whiteout (Log #46)," *Shackleton London* (Dec. 20, 2018), *https://shackletonlondon.com/blogs/lou-s-journal/ into-the-whiteout-log-46*

279   "really methodical," Louis Rudd, "Into the Whiteout (Log #46)," *Shackleton London* (Dec. 20, 2018), *https://shackletonlondon.com/blogs/lou-s-journal/ into-the-whiteout-log-46*

280   "Great considering the conditions." Louis Rudd, "Into the Whiteout (Log #46)," *Shackleton London* (Dec. 20, 2018), *https://shackletonlondon.com/blogs/lou-s-journal/ into-the-whiteout-log-46*

281   "On days like . . . unpleasant start to the day." Louis Rudd, "Into the Whiteout (Log #46)," *Shackleton London* (Dec. 20, 2018), *https://shackletonlondon.com/blogs/lou-s-journal/ into-the-whiteout-log-46*

282   "I reckon I've . . . so they stay up." Louis Rudd, "Furthest in 3000 Miles (Log #47)," *Shackleton London* (Dec. 21, 2018), *https://shackletonlondon.com/blogs/lou-s-journal/ furthest-in-3000-miles-log-47*

283   "fresh food . . . I'm really missing." Louis Rudd, "Dreaming of Food (Log #49)," *Shackleton London* (Dec. 23, 2018), *https://shackletonlondon.com/blogs/lou-s-journal/ dreaming-of-food-log-49*

284   "low cloud on . . . a hugely emotional moment." Louis Rudd, "Carrying Henry's Flag (Log #50)," *Shackleton London* (Dec. 24, 2018), *https://shackletonlondon.com/blogs/lou-s-journal/ henrys-flag-log-50*

285   "It's really important . . . And it will." Louis Rudd, "Carrying Henry's Flag (Log #50)," *Shackleton London* (Dec. 24, 2018), *https://shackletonlondon.com/blogs/lou-s-journal/ henrys-flag-log-50*

286   "the beginning of the end." Louis Rudd, "Carrying Henry's Flag (Log #50)," *Shackleton London* (Dec. 24, 2018), *https://shackletonlondon.com/blogs/lou-s-journal/ henrys-flag-log-50*

287   "Fantastic. Well done to him." Louis Rudd, "Skiing Down Leverett (Log #53)," *Shackleton London* (Dec. 27, 2018), *https://shackletonlondon.com/blogs/lou-s-journal/ skiing-down-leverett-log-53*

288   "For me . . . in race mode." Louis Rudd, "Skiing Down Leverett (Log #53)," *Shackleton London* (Dec. 27, 2018), *https://shackletonlondon.com/blogs/lou-s-journal/ skiing-down-leverett-log-53*

289   "Hopefully I've done . . . to the far side." Louis Rudd, "The Finish (Part One—Log #55)," *Shackleton London* (Dec. 29, 2018), *https://shackletonlondon.com/blogs/lou-s-journal/ the-finish-log-55*

290   "The goal was . . . topsy-turvy be imagined?" Roald Amundsen, *The South Pole: An Account of the Norwegian Antarctic Expedition in the "Fram," 1910–1912*, p. 153.

291   "We are weak . . . the heart of every Englishman." Robert Scott, *Scott's Last Journey*, pp. 179–180.

292   "on the way to . . . comfortable home it was." Roald Amundsen, *The South Pole: An Account of the Norwegian Antarctic Expedition in the "Fram," 1910–1912*, p. 168.

293   "One positively started . . . new human voice." Roald Amundsen, *The South Pole: An Account of the Norwegian Antarctic Expedition in the "Fram," 1910–1912*, p. 174.

294   "showed unmistakable signs . . .

contact with water." Roald Amundsen, *The South Pole: An Account of the Norwegian Antarctic Expedition in the "Fram," 1910–1912*, p. 174.

295 "Capt. Amundsen's Full Story of His Dash to the South Pole with Four of His Men and 18 Dogs." Roald Amundsen, "Crosses Ice Barrier and Reaches the Goal in Fifty-five Days.; AT POLE DEC. 14, 3 P.M." *New York Times* (March 9, 1912), *https://timesmachine.nytimes.com/times-machine/1912/03/09/104893405.html?pageNumber=1*

296 "Amundsen Knows Nothing of Scott." Baker, "Amundsen Knows Nothing of Scott," *New York Times* (March 9, 1912), *http://timesmachine.nytimes.com/times-machine/1912/03/09/104893405.html?pageNumber=1*

297 "To say it . . . cannot express it." Apsley Cherry-Garrard, *The Worst Journey in the World*, p. 468.

298 "we never realized . . . physically, until now." Apsley Cherry-Garrard, *The Worst Journey in the World*, p. 470.

299 "learnt that Amundsen . . . no importance whatever." Apsley Cherry-Garrard, *The Worst Journey in the World*, p. 470.

300 "nobody could hold . . . dangers of the trip." Roald Amundsen, *My Life as an Explorer*, 71.

301 "Is life worth risking for a feat, or losing for your country?" Cherry-Garrard answered as he knew Scott must have: "To face a thing . . . an additional object—knowledge." Apsley Cherry-Garrard, *The Worst Journey in the World*, p. 562.

302 "side-issue . . . in the slightest degree." Roald Amundsen, *The South Pole: An Account of the Norwegian Antarctic Expedition in the "Fram," 1910–1912*, p. 22.

303 "This has been . . . my proudest accomplishment." Colin O'Brady, *Instagram* (Dec. 30, 2018), *https://www.instagram.com/p/BsCcCSmFD6K/*

304 "But what we . . . I'll be happy." Louis Rudd, "Post-Expedition Reflection," *Louis Rudd MBE* (Jan. 14, 2019), *https://lourudd.com/2019/01/14/post-expedition-reflection/*

305 "a minor miracle that both of us have completed." Louis Rudd, "For the Final Time . . . Onwards (Log #54)," *Shackleton London* (Dec. 28, 2018), *https://shackletonlon-don.com/blogs/lou-s-journal/for-the-final-time-onwards-log-54*

306 "my personal food was more or less gone." Adam Skolnick, "Reflections on Antarctica," *New York Times* (Jan. 18, 2019), *https://www.nytimes.com/2019/01/18/sports/reflections-on-antarctica.html*

307 "Congratulations, Ben!" Tim Neville, "Colin O'Brady Wants to Tell You a Story," *Outside Online* (Aug. 15, 2019), *https://www.outsideonline.com/2400795/colin-obrady-profile-antarctica*

308 "half expecting . . . there waiting." Adam Skolnick, "Reflections on Antarctica," *New York Times* (Jan. 18, 2019), *https://www.nytimes.com/2019/01/18/sports/reflections-on-antarctica.html*

309 "popped through . . . Ross Ice Shelf." Colin O'Brady, *Instagram* (Dec. 30, 2018), *https://www.instagram.com/p/BsCcCSmFD6K/*

310 "anti-climax." Louis Rudd, "Post-Expedition Reflection," *Louis Rudd MBE* (Jan. 14, 2019), *https://lourudd.com/2019/01/14/post-expedition-reflection/*

311 "underlying sadness . . . to a close." Colin O'Brady, *Instagram* (Dec. 30, 2018), *https://www.instagram.com/p/BsCcCSmFD6K/*

312 "I've been staggered . . . interest it's generated," Louis Rudd, "Post-Expedition Reflection," *Louis Rudd MBE* (Jan. 14, 2019), *https://lourudd.com/2019/01/14/post-expedition-reflection/*

313 "she gave me . . . without it." Howard Calvert, "This guy just became the first person to cross Antarctica solo and unaided," *Red Bull* (Feb. 4, 2019), *https://www.redbull.com/gb-en/how-colin-o-brady-became-first-person-to-cross-antarctica-solo*

314 "Yes, it . . . finish first." Louis Rudd, "Post-Expedition Reflection," *Louis Rudd MBE* (Jan. 14, 2019), *https://lourudd.com/2019/01/14/post-expedition-reflection/*

315 "It's all about the journey." Adam Skolnick, "Louis Rudd Completes His Trek Across Antarctica 2 Days Behind Colin O'Brady," *New York Times* (Dec. 28, 2018), *https://www.nytimes. com/2018/12/28/sports/louis-rudd-antarctica-colin-obrady.html*

316 "it's a churned up . . . deal breaker!" Louis Rudd, "Post-Expedition Reflection," *Louis Rudd MBE* (Jan. 14, 2019), *https:// lourudd.com/2019/01/14/ post-expedition-reflection/*

317 "not impossible, and it's not the first." Davey Braun, "Alone Across Antarctica Part 3: Nowhere to Hide—Børge Ousland's World Record Legacy," *Outdoor Journal* (July 17, 2019), *https://www.outdoorjournal.com/ featured/athletes-and-explorers/ borge-ousland-antarctica-legacy/*

318 "exceptionally inspirational to me." Rich Roll, "Doing the Impossible with Colin O'Brady," *Rich Roll Podcast* (May 6, 2019), *https://www.youtube.com/ watch?v=10xhj49PUvo*

319 "like comparing apples . . . across an ocean." Mark Synnott, "Free Solo Across Antarctica," *National Geographic* (Nov. 2, 2018), *https://www.nationalgeo-graphic.com/adventure/2018/11/*

antarctica-solo-unaided-cross-ski-attempt-colin-obrady/

320 "I just smile and move on." Davey Braun, "Alone Across Antarctica Part 1: Unbreakable Colin O'Brady Achieves the Impossible Once Again," *Outdoor Journal* (July 10, 2019), *https://www. outdoorjournal.com/featured/un-breakable-colin-obrady-antarctica-world-record/*

321 "probably couldn't do . . . performance athlete." Davey Braun, "Alone Across Antarctica Part 2: Captain Louis Rudd—For the Love of the Journey," *The Outdoor Journal* (July 15, 2019), *https://www.outdoorjournal.com/ featured/athletes-and-explorers/cap-tain-louis-rudd-antactica-crossing/*

322 "It's just a matter of time." Louis Rudd, "Post-Expedition Reflection," *Louis Rudd MBE* (Jan. 14, 2019), *https://lourudd.com/2019/01/14/ post-expedition-reflection/*

323 "a hobby." Louis Rudd, "Post-Expedition Reflection," *Louis Rudd MBE* (Jan. 14, 2019), *https:// lourudd.com/2019/01/14/ post-expedition-reflection/*

324 "Onwards." Louis Rudd, expedition blogs, *Shackleton London, https:// shackletonlondon.com/blogs/ lou-s-journal*

INDEX

Page numbers in *italics* indicate photographs or illustrations.

KEEP READING FOR A SNEAK PEEK OF REBECCA'S NEXT
EDGE-OF-YOUR SEAT NONFICTION THRILLER

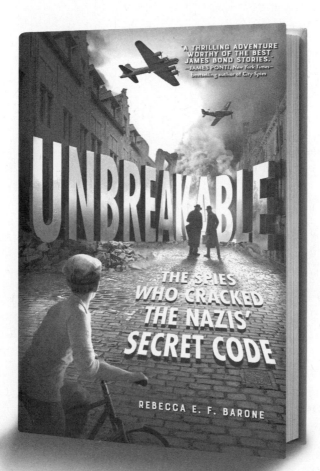

ONE

TRAITOR

1929—Warsaw, Poland

THE BOX ARRIVED on the last Saturday in January.

Business in the Polish customs office went on as usual, the rhythm of sorting and inspecting undisturbed by the heavy package with a German postmark. In fact, the officer in charge had nearly finished when the urgent request came in.

Return it immediately, the German embassy demanded. There had been a mistake. It was a German package, intended for a German recipient. It should never have been sent to Poland. Cease operations and give it back.

Now, *that* made the customs officer pause.

He did not return the box. He opened it.

A polished surface gleamed in the light. Along a hinge in the back, a wood cover opened to reveal something almost like a typewriter. Elevated keys were arranged in three rows along the bottom, each labeled with a letter of the German alphabet.

But that was where the similarity to a typewriter ended.

There was no inked ribbon, no carriage in which to hold paper to type a letter. Instead, the top of the box was filled with small circular windows arranged in three rows identical to the keyboard below; each window contained a single letter printed on translucent material.

If the customs officer pressed a key, instantly, in the top rows, one letter began to glow. As soon as he released the key, the light went out. If he pressed the same letter key again, an entirely different light and letter shone back.

Quickly, the Polish customs officer made a call. Across town, two men secretly working for the Polish cipher agency understood immediately and rushed to the customs office.

Over the next two days and through the next two nights, the men disassembled, examined, and reassembled the machine.

By Monday morning, they had meticulously put every part back into place. They repackaged the machine in the same box and wrapped it in the same brown paper in which it had arrived.

Poland would return German property to Germany, as requested. The delay, inevitable, due simply to the weekend.

No one in Germany suspected a thing.

Enigma in use.
[Bundesarchiv, Bild 183–2007–0705–502 / Walther / CC-BY-SA 3.0]

Two years later, Sunday, November 1, 1931—the
German-Belgian border

Hans-Thilo Schmidt rushed through the doors of the Grand Hotel in Verviers, Belgium, two hours late. He never saw the man sitting in the lobby waiting for him.

To this man, Schmidt was an ordinary German of average build, wearing a dark hat and dark coat. Schmidt was red in the face and puffy around the eyes, both traits the man watching him had been expecting. He knew that Schmidt's train was late, and Schmidt sweated and grew flushed as he hurried to make up lost time. Schmidt's puffy eyes had been expected as well. The people this man watched often suffered from sleepless nights. Treason was never an easy decision.

Not that Schmidt would have noticed the man even if he'd been relaxed and alert. Hans-Thilo Schmidt was far from experienced in spy craft. Last June, when he had first decided to trade secrets for money, he simply walked into the French embassy in Berlin. Incredibly, he plainly announced his intent to sell information to the French government. Without cover and without any personal security, he asked whom he should contact in Paris to do so. Somehow, he had neither been arrested by the Germans nor ignored by the French.

Now, five months later, the German Schmidt was about to meet face-to-face with a French intelligence officer. Hans-Thilo was nervous, and he was late.

At the front desk, the receptionist checked Schmidt into a room already reserved for him and handed him an envelope along with his key. He entered the elevator, and as the doors closed in front of him, the man watching him from the lobby saw him rip into the letter, which read "You are expected in suite 31, first floor, at 12 noon."

At precisely noon, as the letter instructed, Schmidt knocked at suite 31.

The door opened into another world where time seemed to slow as an older woman with elegantly styled white hair greeted him and asked him to wait in the comfortable, richly furnished room. Soft music played gently over the radio. An inviting arrangement of liquor and crystal glasses was set out next to a display of fine cigars. Gratefully, Schmidt eased himself into a plush chair.

"Guten Morgen, Herr Schmidt! Hatten sie eine gute Reise?"

Schmidt jumped as an unfamiliar voice boomed at him in German. An immense man with a shaved head came through a doorway, entering the living area through another room in the suite. Round, dark spectacles framed icy blue eyes that pierced Schmidt with an unwavering stare.

"Sit down, please," the man continued. "How are Madame Schmidt and your two children?"

Schmidt, already on edge, tensed more. He was currently living alone, and his wife, son, and daughter were living with his wife's parents.

"I know," the man said, cutting Schmidt off before he had a chance to answer. "You will want to bring your family back together soon and resume a pleasant life. That, of course, depends on you. We will assist you if your cooperation proves fruitful to us."

Taking an offered glass of whiskey, Schmidt sat back down.

The man confronting him became even more serious. "Your resourcefulness last June in Berlin was quite exceptional and effective, Mr. Schmidt. Quite fortunately you happened upon an official of the French embassy who . . . was inconspicuous. What would you have done if he had thought you were an agent provocateur and called the police?"

This pushed Hans-Thilo Schmidt to his limit. "I thought you would understand!" he snapped, defiant. "If you feel this way, my only option is to withdraw. Others will know how to interpret my motivations and the rationale of my propositions."

"Easy now, Mr. Schmidt," the man responded. "We appreciate your initiative and the benefit we can gain from it.

"Let me be frank," the man continued, "my name is Lemoine, and I represent the French Intelligence Bureau."

Rodolphe Lemoine was the top recruiter and handler for the Deuxième Bureau, the branch of French military intelligence charged with keeping an eye on hostile countries. He was an expert at bringing "assets," people with information and secrets that France needed, into agreement.

One of Lemoine's colleagues had described him as "an amazing person who knows as much about how to compromise a minister as he does recruiting a general. He's as much able to get his hands on a safe as acquire a Yugoslavian passport for you in twenty-four hours."

"That is to say," the same colleague had continued, "you must keep your eyes open and ensure you are not ensnared by the undeniable charm of the man." To Lemoine, another person's weakness was a benefit to be exploited, and he used every advantage, both those that were legal and those that were perhaps not.

This world of secrets and spies was, Lemoine felt, a line of work that benefited from a display of opulence. Money spoke of confidence. And confidence made people comfortable. Comfortable enough, Lemoine knew, to betray their country.

Today's meeting was typical of Lemoine's style: the largest suite, in the most expensive hotel, stocked with fine liquor and large cigars.

"You must have undoubtedly understood," Lemoine continued to Hans-Thilo Schmidt, "that we would have already performed a background check on you. Tell me in detail who you are, what you do, and why you are turning to us. . . . But first, would you like another glass of whiskey?"

With a topped-off glass and now a cigar, Schmidt pulled out his identity cards in silence.

SCHMIDT, HANS-THILO
BORN MAY 13, 1888

Occupation: Beamter im höheren Dienst, Chiffrierstelle
[senior civil servant at the German cipher office]

Whiskey before lunch loosened Schmidt's tongue, and he began to speak.

He had not always been poor. His mother had been born a baroness. He had married a wealthy woman, and his in-laws gave him a house and some land just outside of Berlin as a wedding present. But then Germany's economy declined, and the money went with it. Even with a university degree, finding a career as a chemist was impossible as Germans throughout the country all scrambled for jobs and money. His injuries from the First World War eliminated any possibility of a position as a soldier, too.

Hans-Thilo's brother, on the other hand, was quickly rising through the military ranks, and he managed to use his influence to find Hans-Thilo a job as the assistant to the head of the German cipher office. Mostly, Hans-Thilo arranged appointments and kept track of paperwork. Yet he freely came and went through his commander's office. An office that contained a safe.

It was widely known that the Germans had developed a new type of cipher. Not that anyone in Germany had said as much; they didn't need to. It had become obvious the moment the rest of the world had stopped being able to read their transmissions.

For years, nothing had worked to break the new code; they had never seen a cipher like it before. The Germans were using a mechanical device—the Enigma machine—to rearrange letters of a message into an untraceable pattern. The result was a cipher more complex than any before it. No one could break the German Enigma.

Decoding the cipher and accessing all of the political and military intelligence within its messages would give an enormous advantage to anyone opposing Germany. And though there was currently a fragile peace in Europe—it had been over a decade since the end of WWI—signs of war were once again on the horizon.

As a German, Schmidt knew that other countries, France chief among them, were greedy for help from someone on the inside. Someone like him.

The safe in his commander's office held all the information needed to crack the Enigma cipher: manuals, schematics, codebooks, updates, and plans. Hans-Thilo had access to it all, and he was prepared to deliver it to France. For the right price, of course.

Schmidt's salary could never cover anything more than living expenses. And Schmidt had many debts.

"I've been desperate," he said, finally answering Lemoine's question. "Believe me, Mr. Lemoine, the reliability of our Enigma is total, absolute."

Lemoine knew enough to agree.

"Return here next Sunday with as much intelligence as you're able to provide," said Lemoine. "How much do you earn now?"

"Five hundred Reichsmarks a month."

"Here is triple that amount to compensate you for this first assignment, and to assist you with getting back here on Sunday."

The value of the intelligence Schmidt brought next weekend would determine how much he would be paid then.

Rodolphe Lemoine arrived back in Verviers the next Saturday, one day ahead of Schmidt, and he did not come alone. If Schmidt really did bring information as substantial as he had claimed, Lemoine needed to be prepared. This time, the Deuxième Bureau had also sent a photographer as well as a senior officer, Captain Gustave Bertrand.

Bertrand had spent his life around codebreaking, though he couldn't untangle a cipher to save his life. He preferred to learn secrets a more discreet way. By enabling agents and spies, forging alliances, and purchasing foreign codebooks outright, Bertrand helped to break codes without sitting behind a desk. Lemoine had promised him a windfall.

The next morning, they waited. While Lemoine was downstairs, "settled in like a prince, as usual, in suite 31," Bertrand and the photographer stayed in the two other, much smaller and simpler, rooms.

Schmidt was due at nine o'clock.

Finally, at ten, the phone in Bertrand's room rang.

"We apologize for the delay," Lemoine said. "Can you come down?"

Bertrand rushed out, anxious and impatient, while the photographer stayed with the equipment.

Cigar smoke filled the room, and Schmidt again held a glass of whiskey. When Lemoine made introductions, Schmidt bowed to Bertrand. Though Schmidt wore old, worn-out clothes and dingy shoes, Bertrand remembered that "his blue eyes were beautiful, they shone with intelligence."

"Mr. Barsac," Lemoine began, calling Bertrand by his alias, "you are, I believe, going to be satisfied. Mr. Schmidt did not hesitate to entrust us with a few documents."

Schmidt insisted that he had meant to bring more, too. The list of daily settings for the Enigma, called keys, was usually in his commander's safe, "but my chief left it with one of my colleagues for binding, and I dare not ask for it." He promised to bring it next time.

Lemoine handed Bertrand a folder, thick with hundreds of documents. "He will need them back by no later than 3 P.M. in order to catch the train back to Berlin."

Bertrand took the stairs up to his room three at a time. While the photographer recorded every page, Bertrand read the material. Each sheet was marked GEHEIM—SECRET—and for good reason; Schmidt's documents explained exactly how to set up and operate the German army's Enigma machine.

Before he had left the room, Bertrand had pulled Lemoine aside to discuss payment for their newest spy. At first, Bertrand suggested 5,000 Reichsmarks (about $63,000 in 2022), nearly a full year's salary at Schmidt's regular job. Lemoine, sensing just how excited and impressed Bertrand was, immediately doubled the amount, with the same to be paid again if Schmidt continued to bring information. It was an expensive exchange, but everyone walked away from the meeting satisfied.

Lemoine had his spy. Bertrand had his information.

And Schmidt now had a code name: Asché.

Hundreds of stolen documents! More to come! Bertrand returned to the Deuxième Bureau triumphant. Later, he wrote that Schmidt had just provided him with "the thread that would permit us to get to the heart of the Enigma mystery."

But Bertrand had not fully grasped the complexity of Enigma.

Codebreakers at the Deuxième Bureau had already worked for years to translate Enigma messages. Their efforts had met with so little success that one of Bertrand's colleagues summed it up: "Mechanical encryption is impenetrable. Why waste any time on it?"

When Bertrand returned to Paris and handed over the photographs of the manuals, the material did not change the codebreakers' minds. It was secret information, sure, but it wasn't enough to decipher Enigma messages. Schmidt's manuals explained how to encode messages, not how to read anything that had been intercepted. There wasn't even enough information to explain how to re-create the Enigma from scratch. Without an Enigma machine in hand, this new information was useless.

Crushed but not defeated, Bertrand decided to see if the information could help his colleagues in England. He gave the secret documents to the French station of the British intelligence service. The codebreakers there read the assembled set and even sent the photographs to other codebreakers back home in England.

The verdict stood: Schmidt's information was not enough to break Enigma. The English and the French had given up.

But Bertrand knew there was one more country, one more cipher bureau, that was particularly interested in Enigma.

Bertrand began packing for Poland.

TWO

THE STARTING LINE

December 1931—Warsaw, Poland

POLAND HAD TROUBLE brewing on either side. Sandwiched between Germany to the west and the communist threat of the Soviet Union (USSR) to the east, it was imperative that Poland understand what its enemies were thinking and planning.

"The only ones who are truly passionate about these [cryptography] problems are the Poles," Captain Gustave Bertrand later said.

Now, standing in front of the Saxon Palace in Warsaw, holding his diplomatic bag filled with Asché's documents firmly in hand, Bertrand put his last hope in his friends at the Polish cipher office.

At the palace, grand arches and columns framed a courtyard around the Tomb of the Unknown Soldier. Lawns and hedges sprawled beyond the colonnade, joining the two buildings of the Polish General Staff, the highest offices of the Polish armed forces. Inside, Major Gwido Langer was waiting.

Bertrand wore the small half smile of a man prone to keeping secrets; Langer carried himself with the intense, confident posture of a man used to exploiting any weakness.

Twice, while a soldier during the First World War and in the skirmishes that followed, Langer had become a prisoner of war. He had escaped, too, and had trekked hundreds of miles through

Siberia to rejoin his army. Langer's bravery had become apparent during these wars, but so, too, had his grasp of military strategy; he witnessed and understood how decrypting intelligence had changed defeat to victory in key battles. It made such an impression that Langer devoted the rest of his life to ensuring that Poland could break other countries' codes and access their information. By 1929, Langer had become the head of the Polish cipher office—all of Polish counterintelligence that touched codebreaking was under his command.

And now Bertrand said he had something new.

Inside the Saxon Palace, Bertrand pulled out the photographs. He laid Enigma manuals and instructions in front of Langer. Were they really as worthless as the French and British had said?

Langer took one look, and immediately there was "an explosion of amazement and joy," Bertrand remembered. As soon as he collected himself, Langer rushed out of the room and returned with two colleagues.

"This is extraordinary and unexpected!" one of the Polish codebreakers cried.

Bertrand let them have forty-eight hours to examine the documents. Two days later, when the Frenchman returned to the Saxon Palace, Langer and his colleagues were waiting. "They were radiant," remembered Bertrand. "The Schmidt documents were welcomed like manna in the desert."

"Vous avez fait donner l'artillerie lourde!" ["You brought out the big guns!"] Langer said, not mincing words. "This is crucial for the future of our research. We cannot express enough our gratitude."